Dealing with Dyslexia

'Parents never teach their children language without the latter, by themselves, inventing language along with them.'

Johan Gottfried Herder, Essay on the Origin of Language (1772), translated by J.M. Moran and A. Gode

Dealing with Dyslexia

Second Edition

Pat Heaton and Patrick Winterson

Consultant in Dyslexia: Professor Margaret Snowling,
University of York

Whurr Publishers

© 1996 Whurr Publishers Ltd
First published 1996 by
Whurr Publishers Ltd
19b Compton Terrace, London N1 2UN, England

British Library Cataloguing in Publication Data
A catalogue record for this book is available from the British Library

ISBN 1-897635-57-5

Printed and bound in the UK by Athenaeum Press Ltd, Gateshead, Tyne & Wear

Contents

Appendices

About the authors

Pat Heaton has been screening and teaching dyslexics of all ages for more then 20 years. A first degree qualification in linguistics inspired interest in language-disabled pupils and this led to a Masters degree course in dyslexia at Bangor University. Pat is also a graduate member of the British Psychological Society and a co-course director of the RSA Diploma in Specific Learning Difficulties. Published works include *Learning to Learn, Parents in Need* and the *Pam and Tom Reading Scheme.*

Patrick Winterson read English literature at Cambridge and subsequently took an MA in Linguistics under Professor Randolph Quirk. He has taught in two state secondary schools but his career has been spent mainly in teaching linguistics to teachers in training and other adults. He has published two introductory texts-with-tape on linguistic topics.

Acknowledgements

Our thanks are due to many people who have helped in the production of this book and especially to Professor T.R. Miles, David Brazil and Ken Reah who generously gave the time needed to read an earlier version of the text and made many valuable suggestions. For errors and indiscretions which nevertheless remain we are, of course, responsible. Our thanks are also due to M. Butler and V. Parkin for the ideas and designs of some of the games and to those who have kindly permitted us to reproduce material from current works: to the Invalid Children's Aid Association for an extract from A. Wolff's paper which is included in the book entitled *The Assessment and Teaching of Dyslexic Children*, to Susan Hampshire for permission to make extensive reference to her book *Susan's Story* and to Messrs. Heinemann for the many references to Hornsby and Shear's structured language programme, *Alpha to Omega*.

We must also express our gratitude to our families, friends, pupils and their parents who have helped us at all stages of the work, not forgetting, of course Dr Bevé Hornsby.

How to use this book

Parents and others who are confronted with an emergency situation calling for immediate action should turn at once to Book Two - 'immediate problems and strategies'.

Book Two should be supplemented as soon as possible by a reading of Book One (for background) and Book Three (for information). Readers whose interest in dyslexia is mainly professional and academic should read straight through.

Symbols

Throughout the book, slashes(//) are used to make it clear when phonemic symbols are being employed to focus attention on words as *sounds*, as for instance to highlight the *pronounciation* of 'cat' as /kæt/.

Pointed brackets(<>) are used when it is desired to focus attention on words as *visible* objects: thus <caught> and <court> can both represent the spoken word /kɔt/.

By extension '/word/' is shorthand for 'spoken word' and '<word>' stands for 'written word'.

A complete list of the symbols used is printed as Appendix C and also inside the back cover for ready reference.

Introduction

Preliminary remarks

The nine years since the first appearance of *Dealing with Dyslexia* have been marked by interesting and even dramatic developments in experimental and academic work associated with early reading. Some of this work has already begun to affect teaching methods. In general it has been characterised by a welcome increase in linguistic awareness and sophistication (see p. xv) which is very much in line with the approach adopted, developed and advocated by us in the first edition. However, things have not stood still since 1986 and it is now necessary to consider how to take account of more recent developments without, in the process, blurring the outlines of our original presentation. In general, it has seemed best to interfere as little as possible with running text and footnotes (though alterations and annotations have been made where necessary) and to deal with more recent work in a separate treament, first by providing an additional select list of works consulted for the new edition and, second, by offering these introductory remarks.

Select list of works consulted for the second edition

This appears on p. 230–1 and refers to 30 books, papers and other formulations. The shift of scholarly emphasis referred to above which has been brought about largely through the work there listed has also brought to our attention other relevant material which was appearing, or had already appeared, when the first edition was in preparation. The new select list deals in some depth with recent research and discussion (which has been focused largely on developmental psychology) in some depth and is therefore suitable for the reader who wishes to be aware of source material; the general bibli-ography remains for those interested in the wider background. For readers in both categories, Snowling and Thomson (1991) and Goswami and Bryant (1990) can be recommended for comprehensive surveys of the current state of play.

Language takes centre stage

In Chapter 3 of the original edition (Developmental dyslexia, cause and effect), we considered the approach adopted by behavioural psychologists and drew attention to what appeared to be two major defects in the existing research: first, it left the general reader with an impression that was 'both fragmented and confused'; second, it suffered from 'an inability to come to grips with the fundamental nature of the topic. Instead of recognising reading and writing as unique activities flowing from a unique human capability, behavioural research (had) tended to treat them as though they were no different from other activities requiring precise visual and muscular control'. (First edition, p. 28)

These remarks drew on conclusions already reached by Frank Vellutino in his model study *Dyslexia Theory and Research* (1979) and by Michael Stubbs in *Language and Literacy* (1980). Stubbs had written of a

> ... general failure, in much of the experimental psychological literature, to regard reading and writing as *linguistic* processes. Reading has often been seen predominantly as a matter of visual processing, involving characteristic eye movements, perceptual span, word gestalts and so on. As a result it has often been ignored that what people read is linguistically organised and meaningfully structured.

In 1982, Isabel Liberman1 could still write in the epic vein of her struggle as a 'lonely warrior' against dark forces of 'optometrists armed with wooden beads and trampolines' for whom reading was an exercise in visual perception and muscular co-ordination, and against psychologists who perceived it as a 'psycholinguistic guessing game' in which the reader sprang 'directly from print to meaning'. Liberman went on to point out that what the reader 'perceives' is not just 'print' but an *orthography*, and that what an (alphabetic) orthography represents is, 'not the thing itself... but the language'. Decoding an orthography was therefore not a matter of muscular co-ordination, visual perception or guesswork, but one of *'dealing in distinctively linguistic ways with units of language'* (our italics). It followed that 'the first requirement for beginning readers' (and for psychologists?) was 'to acquire a certain amount of linguistic sophistication'.

By then, the tide was already setting strongly in a new direction and, in 1986, Shankweiler and Crain[2] could resoundingly '*take it for granted*' that 'the deficiences of most children who develop reading problems reflect limitations *in the language area* and not in general cognitive limitations of perception' (our italics). The psychologists had finally caught up with the linguists and arrived at the position summarised by us, also in 1986, in the proposition (p. 22) that 'Dyslexia is what it appears to be – an impairment of **language** ...making itself manifest through the processes which underlie writing, reading and the production of speech.' (See also the general argument of Chapters 3, 4 and 5.)

Also 'taken for granted' by Shankweiler and Crain was the view (from neural network theory) that the human language apparatus forms a biologically-coherent or 'evolved' system, 'distinguished from other parts of the cognitive apparatus by special brain structures and other anatomical specialisations' and hence, in our terms (see pp. 30, 31 and the whole argument of Chapter 2), 'available to be disrupted'. This assumption has argumentative significance for normal and disadvantaged readers, because it carries with it the clear implication that human language is 'there' to be 'known'; and leads in turn to such interesting and reasonable questions as: How does the knowledge about language that a reader has differ from the knowledge that a speaker has? What steps need to be taken in order to acquire that kind of knowledge? and How might that process differ in normal and handicapped readers?

Segmentation – José Morais

The debate about the kind of indirect (meta-linguistic) knowledge-about-language that readers are supposed to acquire and use has tended to focus especially on the question of *segmentation*, since spoken language is essentially a *continuous* stream of sound, while written signs of whatever kind are by their nature *discontinuous*, so that the inventors of a writing system (and perhaps each young reader of it) have to arrive at an analysis, or *segmentation*, of speech into discontinuous elements that are then to be provided with a rational system of visible labels. The elements to be so labelled have, at different times and places, been located at different stages of the linguistic edifice, variously at the level of 'idea', morpheme, syllable, phoneme or some combination or blend of those four. It was natural to enquire whether such activity called on meta-linguistic knowledge and, if so, whether there was any way in which such knowledge could be reinforced.

José Morais sparked off a lively and productive debate by his demonstration (1979) that the ability to analyse the continuous stream of spoken language into 'separate' sounds ('phonemic awareness') which underlies the operation of an *alphabetic* orthography was not, as had been assumed, a *prerequisite* for the development of alphabetic reading but a *consequence* of it. His finding that adult illiterates were unable to perform tasks calling for (oral) phonemic[3] segmentation was subsequently reinforced by studies of Chinese and Japanese students who had learned to read in a non-alphabetic writing system. Put in simple terms (and there has been some considerable adjustment of positions since 1979), this conclusion appeared to invalidate the whole notion of 'phonic' approaches to reading, since such methods implied that the teacher had taken on the 'impossible'[4] task of developing a pre-reading skill which could only emerge *after* reading had been acquired. It then became something of a puzzle that reading could ever have been taught at all, since methods of teaching have been from time immemorial explicitly or implicitly phonic.

One could also wonder how a phoneme–grapheme orthography could have been invented in the first place by people who were, by definition, pre-literate. On the other side (and in favour of Morais' argument), was the persuasive and independent evidence suggesting that beginning readers make very little use of sound–symbol relationships (see below).

In general and much simplified terms, there are three ways in which one can respond to the claim underlying Morais' 1979 paper and the work deriving from it.

The first approach is to accept that learning to read has to begin in the absence of 'phonemic awareness' and to concentrate the initial pedagogic thrust entirely into various forms of the 'whole word' or 'whole book' method. This is not an unreasonable strategy and there is plenty of evidence to suggest that it works for 'normal readers'. Goswami and Bryant reviewed the research and arrived at the 'uncomfortable' conclusion (1990) that there was 'very little direct evidence that children who are learning to read do rely on letter–sound relationships to help them read words'. Perhaps, after all, many of us do, at some stage, jump 'directly from print to meaning'?

A second reaction to Morais' claim would be to disprove it and this is essentially the direction taken in a series of 'longitudinal' studies starting at the pre-literate stage. Lundberg, Frost and Petersen (1988) provided a group of Danish children who had not yet begun to read with tuition which included work on phonemic segmentation. They were able to demonstrate that this 'impossible' procedure did nevertheless enable the subjects subsequently to outperform a control group of untutored children. The researchers concluded that 'phonemic awareness can be developed among pre-school children outside the context of the acquisition of an alphabetic writing system' which, indeed, 'presupposes the capacity for explicit analysis of speech in terms of phonemes'.

This position, too, is not unreasonable and the two responses are perhaps less contradictory than might at first appear. It may be helpful at this point to draw a rather simple parallel between phonemic awareness and another skill/faculty – that of *balance*. An argument along the lines that walking was the *cause* and not the *product* of balance might well be supported by a demonstration that adults who for some reason had never walked were also lacking in balancing skills. Such skills (it could then be inferred) do not 'arise spontaneously', although they can develop once the possibility of bipedal gait has been restored. Manufacturers of 'baby walkers' could take comfort from the probability that balance and walking were in fact strongly interactive skills that developed each other.

Syllable and rhyme

A third response to the conclusions to be drawn from Morais (1979) is that adopted by Goswami and her associates who, while largely accepting the view that phonemic segmentation does not occur at the pre-literate stage, have still maintained that *segmentation at some level* is both antecedent to, and necessary for, the acquisition of reading. They have gone on to propose the more accessible level of the *syllable* as the point of departure for the process of segmentation and ordering of events which allows children to use their highly developed feeling for *rhymes* and *speech rhythms*, both of which are carried by patternings of syllables. They also believe that rhyme (through the notion of analogy) continues to play an important part in early reading and spelling. (For a full discussion, see Goswami and Bryant (1990), Chapter 4.) This contention, too, is extremely plausible given the strong affinity between children at the pre-reading stage and all forms of exuberant word-play as demonstrated by traditional rhymes like 'Hickory dickory dock'.[5] The importance of intuitions at the syllabic level can, however, be accepted without ruling out the possibility of simultaneous intuitions at other levels. (See also Book Three, Chapter 4, footnote 1, p. 194.)

Conclusion

Reading in an alphabetic orthography is a visual activity mysteriously underpinned and sustained by the sounds of speech through the medium of letters and letter groups. The research briefly reviewed above has begun to reflect this truth more closely than ever before by becoming more linguistically informed and more linguistically coherent. One can now agree with the conclusion (Snowling and Hulme, 1993) that 'research in this field has made massive strides in recent years' and our comment that 'researchers have tended not to have or not to use the insights provided by the science of linguistics' (First edition, p.28) is now in need of qualification (although it is not clear that the new enlightenment has yet found its way to psychologists working in the field).

The fact remains that effective teaching, especially of children with serious reading problems, still continues to demand that teachers and tutors use every possible resource of knowledge and skill, including meta-linguistic skill, and seek to derive something of value even from contradictory streams of research. *Dealing with Dyslexia* was originally written to make the insights of linguistic science available to teachers, tutors and parents through problems of delayed or retarded reading. The necessity for this should now be clearer than ever.

Note

[1]Liberman, I.Y. (1982). A language-oriented view of reading and its disabilities. In Myklebust, H. (Ed.) Progress in Learning Disabilities (Vol. 5, pp. 81-101) Grune and Stratton.

[2]Shankweiler, D. and Crain, S. (1986). Language mechanisms and reading disorder: a modular approach. Cognition, 24: 139–68.

[3]In their 1979 paper Morais et al refer to 'speech as a sequence of phones'.

[4]C.f. Stuart and Coltheart (1988), especially p. 148.

[5]For instance, Bradley and Bryant (1983) propose 'the hypothesis that the awareness of rhyme and alliteration which children acquire before they go to school, possibly as a result of their experience at home, has a powerful effect on their eventual success...

Book One
About dyslexia

Chapter 1
The existence of dyslexia

Dyslexia and Literacy

'Whatever specific Dyslexia may eventually be analysed to be, there is no reason to presuppose that it always occurs in isolation.' Money (1962). *Reading Disability: progress and research needs in dyslexia* (p. 10)

It is extraordinary that in a literate and comparatively wealthy society any young person should be able to complete 10 years of schooling without acquiring a minimum competence in reading and spelling. Yet it was estimated in 1973 that there were then at least 1 million semi-literate adults in the United Kingdom, and a study carried out in 1970/71 concluded that some 15 000 school *leavers* in that year were 'semi-literate' (figures from the *Bullock Report*, 1975, pp. 11–12). More recently (in 1994), the Adult Literacy and Basic Skills Unit estimated that 4% of the adult population of England and Wales (about 2 million) were functionally illiterate.[1]

These figures attract a certain amount of controversy, but it is clear that many young people are failing to become literate and it is far from clear why any at all should fail in this way. We, the authors, do not consider that any kind or level of illiteracy, in adulthood or in late adolescence, is acceptable or should be tolerated, and our concern for the misery and frustration suffered by one group of handicapped readers (and chronicled by several of them) is certainly not to be taken as implying any lack of regard for the others. On the contrary it seems to us that the problems of dyslexics and those of other slow readers are so related and intertwined that they must to an extent be studied and remedied together.

First of all, there is an obvious relationship of *substance*; all types of difficulty manifest themselves in the same area, the area of *visible* (i.e. written or printed) *language* function,[2] and this must necessarily imply some similarity of approach and treatment.

3

Second, there is a relationship of *symptom*. There is no reason why some of those pupils whose reading problems may reasonably be ascribed to social causes or to a generally low level of academic attainment should not exhibit symptoms of dyslexia as well – as of course they often do. For instance, a study of dyslexia in the Isle of Wight suggested a minimum prevalence rate of 4%, while a comparable study in a working-class, inner city area (Camberwell, south-east London) suggested a prevalence rate of 8–9%. 'It has been

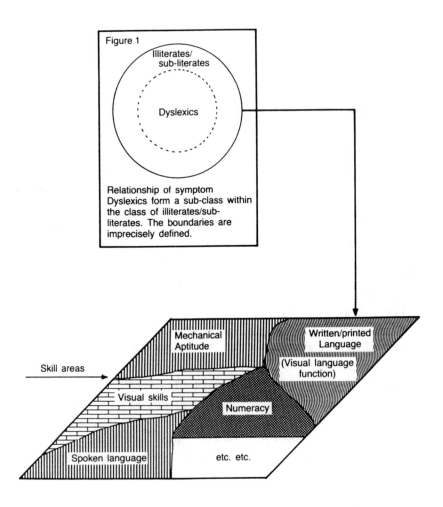

Figure 2. Relationship of substance. All types of difficulty manifest themselves in the same area, that of visual language function. (Figure 1 forms part of Figure 2.)

hypothesised that this discrepancy can be accounted for by the presence of adverse social and environmental factors in the more deprived population; these could be expected to exacerbate the expression of an inherent tendency' (Val Muter, 'The relationship between definitions and assessment in dyslexia', *Dyslexia Review*, Vol. 5, No. 1, summer 1982).

Nevertheless, even though it is not possible to draw a hard and fast methodological or clinical boundary between dyslexics and other disadvantaged readers, it is still possible to distinguish the dyslexic *condition* from that of general reading retardation because dyslexia brings with it an extra dimension of difficulty. Dyslexics have to contend not only with the problems that confront all beginning readers by reason of the sheer complexity of the reading/writing process, but also with those special obstacles that arise from the nature of dyslexia 'in itself'. The dividing line between general and specific language difficulty may not be sharply drawn but it still carries important implications for diagnosis and teaching.

To say all this is to say that whatever the relationship and the proportionality between general and specific handicap, it is clearly the case that in *Dealing with Dyslexia* one is attacking the problems of reading and spelling in their most specific, their most fundamental and their most persistent forms. The concentration and commitment that this demands from teachers, clinicians and researchers alike is in itself an important contribution towards a final understanding and resolution of the wider problems of adult and adolescent illiteracy.

The argument about dyslexia. Causes of illiteracy

Many teachers and parents get on as best they can with the business of helping dyslexic children without troubling themselves overmuch with wider questions. Nevertheless it has to be accepted that the nature and indeed the existence of dyslexia has been a difficult and controversial topic, superimposed as it is upon the highly charged controversies that already surround the teaching of reading. This means that most concerned parents and teachers will sooner or later find themselves having to stand up for their conviction that dyslexia is a real and treatable condition, particularly if they are under the administration of an education authority in which the existence of dyslexia is officially denied. Accordingly, we shall now expose and examine the issues that have been fundamental to the debate.

In the first place, it is obvious that the failure of many children to learn to read, despite long exposure to a school system expressly designed to foster literacy, *calls for some explanation*. A number of explanations have been put forward, or have put themselves forward including, of course, dyslexia. Our next task will be to discuss and compare these explanations and we shall present this part of our argument by reference to an imaginary sample of 12-year-old children who are failing to acquire basic literacy. Figure 3 shows the possible make-up of such a sample.

The diagram states that in a randomly selected group of non-literate 12-year-olds, the failure to acquire literacy could be ascribed to a number of different causes. (*Dyslexia Theory and Research*, Chapter 2, by F.R. Vellutino (1979) contains a full account of the 'extrinsic factors' that might be expected to affect the acquisition of reading.)

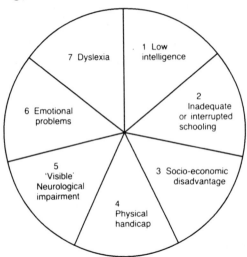

Figure 3. Imaginary sample of children who are failing to acquire literacy, showing possible reasons for failure.

The diagram is oversimplified in two ways; first, because it implies that the causes are equally distributed among the children (the segments are all much the same size) and, second, because it implies that the causes are segregated from one another (located in separate segments). We have no reason to believe either that the causes would be evenly distributed among the children in the sample or that they would be segregated. It is entirely possible for instance, that a child might be affected by emotional problems *and* poor schooling, or by physical handicap *and* low intelligence. Some of the factors may be causally interrelated. We have shown the causes as equal and separate entities purely in order to get a straightforward diagram which the reader must feel free to scramble according to taste.

The causal factors call for some additional comment as follows:

1. Low intelligence. The very mention of intelligence, particularly low intelligence, gives deep offence to many well-intentioned people. Nevertheless, we think it is self-evident that there is such a thing as a generally low level of intellectual ability which might be expected to delay or inhibit the acquisition of literacy.

2. Schooling: a) Inadequate. Poor organisation, or confusion of method, might account for early failure in reading. b) Interrupted. Evidently, interrupted schooling can disrupt the educational process, including the acquisition of literacy.

3. Socio-economic disadvantage. There is a correlation between socio-economic stratum and the acquisition of reading. 'For example, the National Child Development Study revealed that 48% of children from social class V were poor readers at age seven compared with 8% in social class I . . . the position worsens as the children grow older . . .' (*Bullock Report*, 1975, p. 22). A current explanation for this puzzling phenomenon (which is not confined to the UK) is that it is a symptom of 'alienation' felt by some parts of society from a 'dominant culture' which is somehow embodied in the processes of reading and writing. Whether or not there is any truth in this explanation or partial explanation, the negative correlation between socio-economic level and the acquisition of literacy is a factor that should not be glossed over and one which everyone concerned with or about the educational process must wish to change.

4. Physical handicap. A physical handicap (of vision, for instance) might affect the acquisition of literacy directly, or it might work indirectly through interrupted schooling or because of 'stereotyping' which caused the handicapped person to be taught at a level below his or her true potential.

5. 'Visible' neurological impairment. The same applies; a neurological deficit (crudely, 'brain damage') might affect the acquisition of literacy directly or it might indirectly affect the quality of schooling. A 'visible' impairment means one that manifests itself in ways *that go beyond reading and writing*. It is plausible that dyslexia is itself the result of an otherwise unremarked ('invisible') disturbance of neural function.

6. Emotional factors. These include all those psychiatric or behavioural disorders which might affect concentration or attention and hence the ability to benefit from schooling.

7. Dyslexia. This is, of course, the main topic of this book. We shall be considering its characteristics in a later section.

It goes without saying that any of these causes can be mild or severe in its nature or effect.

Visible causation

A general comment to be made about causes 1–6 (i.e. all the causes other than dyslexia) is that they are *visible* – they have a noticeable effect on large areas of personality and performance and not just on reading and writing. Dyslexia, in contrast, is limited in its effects. Generally, only reading and writing (visual language function) are affected, though there may also be some impairment of related subskills. For this reason dyslexia has sometimes been called the 'hidden handicap'. It follows that a theory of reading disability *which dispenses entirely with dyslexia* will be a theory of *visible causation*. We shall employ this as a cover term in the rest of our discussion.

To summarise

If one randomly selected from the general population a group of children aged 12 who were illiterate or severely retarded in reading and spelling, then their problem could be explained in seven different ways or combinations of ways. *Six* of these causes would be unspecific, capable of manifesting themselves *visibly* in broad areas of behaviour which might or might not include reading and writing. *One* of them, on the other hand, is specifically related to performance in visual language.

We can now turn to the question that is central to this whole discussion, namely

Do we need dyslexia?

Suppose that all the cases of retarded reading/spelling in our sample could be explained in terms of causes 1 to 6. Suppose, in other words, that all the children in the sample showed evidence of

Visible Causation ➔

i.e.	
	low intelligence
or	inadequate/interrupted schooling
or	socio-economic disadvantage
or	physical handicap
or	neurological impairment
or	psychological/behavioural problems

or some combination of these causes, then it would be both reaso
able and economical to suggest that the phenomenon of
illiteracy/subliteracy should be accounted for just in terms of these
causes and that dyslexia could and should be banished from the
theory.

Figure 3 would then be redrawn like this:

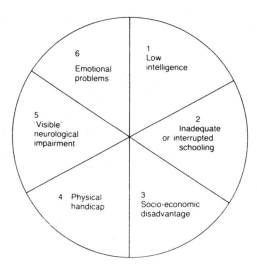

Figure 4. 'Visible causation' of retarded literacy. In the *simplified theory* reading retardation is attributed entirely to these factors, singly or in combination.

The redrawn diagram asserts, in effect, that if all six 'visible' causes could be eliminated or counteracted in the individual or in society at large, then the problems of subliteracy would cease to exist. More formally, the diagram makes the claim that *visible causation* is both a necessary and a sufficient condition for the appearance of reading retardation. If, however, these causes were to be eliminated and yet there still remained individuals in our sample with severe and resistant problems of reading and spelling, then one would have to accept that the 'simplified' theory of causation was inadequate and it would be necessary to resume the search for an 'invisible' factor.

Dyslexia would be back in business.

We shall now consider the argument in further detail.

a. 'Visible causation' is not a *necessary* condition for retarded literacy.
If we put aside our imaginary sample and return to the situation that confronts us in real life, it becomes apparent that there are individuals who display *none* of the causal factors listed in Figure 4 but who still suffer from severe and prolonged, in fact life-long, disturbance of visi-

\6

iction. It was precisely the clinical description of such
rated the modern study of dyslexia. (For instance, W.
account of 'A case of congenital word blindness'
.. the *British Medical Journal* for November 1896.)

_ould be noted that even if only *one* individual could be found
whose reading impairment occurred in the absence of all the visible
causes listed in Figure 4, then that fact in itself would be sufficient to
establish the existence of an additional *invisible* factor which could
conveniently be labelled 'dyslexia'. In fact, however, instances of
reading retardation *without* visible cause, far from being confined to
one or a few individuals, are abundant both in the literature and
within the experience of practitioners. One writer has remarked of
cases where severe and persistent problems occur in people of
normal intelligence and do not appear to be 'due to psychiatric
disorder, social disadvantage or lack of schooling'. '. . . The existence
of children with the problems described by these early workers has
been documented so many times both in clinical practice and
through systematic research . . . that it is unnecessary to review the
evidence here' (Benton and Pearl, 1978, p. 6).

We have already been at pains to insist that dyslexia *need not* occur
in this 'pure' form (and see the quotation at the head of this chapter),
but when it does so occur the individuals concerned are good
evidence for the existence of dyslexia besides being valuable subjects
for systematic study.

b. 'Visible causation' is not a *sufficient* condition for retarded literacy
The *visible* causes listed in Figure 4 apply to the argument in another
way. Having shown that they are not in themselves *necessary* conditions for retarded reading, it remains to point out that they are not
sufficient conditions for retarded reading either since pupils may
exhibit any or all of the 'visible causes' and still become fluent readers. To put the matter in its plainest terms we can state that a person
may become an effective reader even though he or she

1   is of low intelligence
2   has suffered inadequate or interrupted schooling
3   is socio-economically disadvantaged
4   is physically handicapped
5   suffers from visible neurological impairment
6   suffers from emotional problems.

This argument is virtually self-sustaining since a moment's
reflection will confirm that conditions 2 to 6 can, and regularly do,

co-occur with fluent reading. The position is perhaps a little less clear with regard to condition 1, but it is known that people of very low intelligence can become effectively literate. 'Reading has been taught to children of IQ 50 or occasionally even below that level' (Michael Rutter, in Benton and Pearl, 1978).[3] We can cite a report of a girl with a history of hyperthyroidism and an IQ of 59/65 who was reading at the age of eight-and-a-half 'with good word reading and comprehension' (Money, 1962, p. 25).[4] The authors of the *Bullock Report* make a related point when they state '. . . although a number of children in difficulty do have below average test intelligence, some degree of hearing impediment or indeterminate laterality, the same may be said of large numbers of successful readers' (p. 271).

In conclusion

We think that the case for 'visible causation' is very hard to sustain when 'visible factors' are seen to be neither sufficient nor necessary conditions for failure in reading. Before leaving the subject it may be instructive to refer to the somewhat analogous case of the link between smoking and lung cancer. While one would obviously not wish to maintain that there was *no* connection between smoking and cancer of the lung (or between *visible* causes and reading retardation), the fact that

> some non-smokers contract cancer of the lung (smoking not a *necessary* cause)
> while some heavy smokers live to a ripe old age and then die of other diseases (smoking not a *sufficient* cause)

means that some other causative agent *must be at work*.

The overall situation is illustrated in Figure 5. If one imagines a population consisting of all the members of our culture whom we *expect* to be able to read or to have made satisfactory progress in reading, then they might subdivide into three sets that interlock. It is not *necessary* to belong to group b in order to be a 'retarded reader' (because of area c-2), nor is it *sufficient* (because of area a-1).

Dyslexia as a middle-class aberration

The view of dyslexia as a disease of middle-class parents unable to reconcile themselves to the dullness of their offspring has been widespread and even dominant among influential areas of the educational establishment. No doubt it has played its part in reducing the

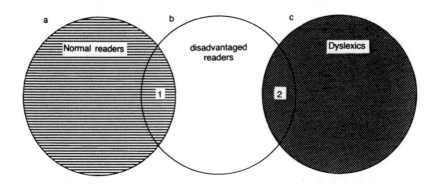

Figure 5 The members of our culture whom we expect to be able to read or to be making satisfactory progress in reading (i.e. not toddlers) fall into three interlocking sets. The circles are not drawn to any particular scale. Membership of group b is neither a necessary (c-2) nor sufficient (a-1) condition for retarded reading. 'Disadvantage does not immunise against Dyslexia' (area 2).

amount of help available to dyslexic children. Nevertheless, it is logically untenable. For it to be true it would have to be the case that children diagnosed as dyslexic were characteristically and overwhelmingly

    a unintelligent
    b middle-class.

Intelligence

Retarded literacy combined with average or above-average IQ has always (rightly or wrongly) been regarded as the leading criterion for identifying a case of dyslexia. Some early workers believed that dyslexia *only* occurred in children of above-average intelligence (as with so-called 'media dyslexics'). However, it is more likely that dyslexics cover much the same range of intelligence as the rest of the population and that dyslexia is not strongly correlated with intelligence one way or the other. It is certainly not correlated with low intelligence.[5]

Class

We have already noted that general reading retardation is correlated with *low* socio-economic status. We would not wish to make the same strong claim for dyslexia which, being a 'developmental' or 'constitutional' condition, is probably unrelated to social class. Evidence for the 'developmental' character of dyslexia will be put forward in subsequent sections. For the moment, we may remark somewhat anecdotally that one of the authors practises in an industrial town and works almost exclusively with dyslexic children whose parents are not 'middle-class', unless this somewhat archaic expression is taken to mean 'concerned about their children's progress, and unwilling to be fobbed off with stereotyped explanations'.

Having said all this, one must concede that there are certain aspects of what might be called the dyslexia scene that make it rather easy to entertain a class-based view of dyslexia, especially if this is congenial for other reasons. The emphasis given to procedures of testing and assessment makes it seem that a child has to *qualify* to be a dyslexic by being in some way 'special' and this idea is certainly acceptable to some parents. To us, it would seem more reasonable and more in accord with the facts that dyslexics should be regarded and treated within the same frame of reference as other slow readers. Certainly, there is nothing in the procedures we are recommending that could be harmful to children with other kinds of reading problem. In fact, these procedures may sometimes be an improvement on what is otherwise available. The dominant influence of procedures for testing and selection is to be ascribed largely to the standard requirement of an official test before a child can receive special help of any kind, and of course diagnostic tests (audiometric tests, for instance) can be invaluable in cases where there is a readily quantifiable disability. Nevertheless, it is still possible to wonder what precisely is expected to be achieved by elaborate test procedures applied to a child with an early reading difficulty.[6]

Is it to establish there is a difficulty? This will already be sufficiently obvious.

Is it to establish the level of the child's intelligence? This is irrelevant; children at all levels of intelligence can be dyslexic and children at all levels of intelligence can, and should, become effectively literate.

Is it to establish within fine limits a precise kind of difficulty? This is impossible and unnecessary. The notion of sharply different *kinds* of dyslexia demanding sharply distinct treatments seems to us to be contrary both to the evidence and to common sense.[7] *One* dyslexia is quite enough for most people to swallow. Individual differences that do exist are best handled within the professional competence of the teacher, helped by contact and co-operation with parents.

What does seem important is that there should be a plentiful supply of teachers both 'public' and 'private' who are well equipped to deal with all kinds of difficulty (with some scope for specialisation of course). Without in any way wishing to denigrate the many excellent teachers who are at work in this field, it does seem reasonable to suspect that their skills could be enhanced by a clearer perception of dyslexia in relation to other causal factors and by access to the insights which linguistics can bring to the subject-matter of their discipline, which is *language* in its spoken and, more especially, in its written form.

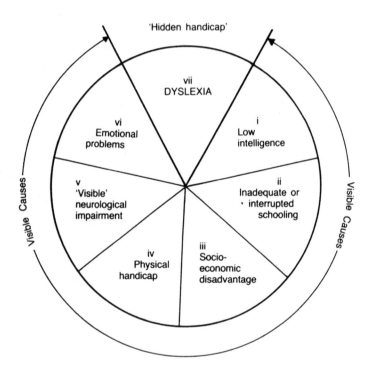

Figure 6. The causes of retarded reading/spelling.

This book sets out to provide that perception and those insights and in so doing to make a distinct step towards the abolition of illiteracy.

We can now reinstate our original diagram with some embellishments.

Notes

[1] A survey of some 12 000 British 23-year-olds carried out in 1981 as part of the National Child Development Study suggested that 'there may be considerably more than 2 million adults in Great Britain whose literacy skills are not sufficient to meet the demands placed upon them' (from *Literacy and Numeracy*, published by the Adult Literacy and Basic Skills Unit, 1983).

A more recent survey (1994) of a representative sample of 3000 adults in England and Wales has tended to confirm these results. For all age groups, the level of illiteracy ('very serious difficulties with reading') amounted to 4%, equating to 2 million people over the whole population. For the 22–24-year-old age group, the figure was 3% (1.5 million people).

If one adds together the percentages for the literacy levels 'very poor' and 'poor', then the figure for all age groups comes to 15% (7.5 million people) and for the 22–24-year-old age group 13% (6.5 million). The Adult Literacy and Basic Skills Unit, which sponsored the survey, concluded that 'standards are not good enough for an industrialised country towards the end of the twentieth century' and called for 'concerted action' to raise levels of performance (data from *Older and Younger: the basic skills of different age groups*, ALBSU, 1995).

[2] 'Visible/visual language' means language made visible. Hence, 'visible/visual language function' means 'the activities of writing and reading', just as 'audible language function' means 'the activities of speaking and hearing'. A difficulty over 'visual language function' does not necessarily imply a failure of eyesight any more than a failure of audible language (for instance, a speech impediment) necessarily implies a failure of hearing.

[3] The research referred to is reported in *Education, Health and Behaviour* by M. Rutter, J. Tizard and K. Whitemore (Longman, 1970).

[4] See also *The Second International Reading Symposium*, edited by John Downing and Amy L, Brown (Cassell, 1967), p. 271.

[5] See also Stanovich (1994) ' ...although genetic and neuro-anatomical studies may be narrowing in on a syndrome of dyslexia, that syndrome does not seem to be strongly correlated with degree of IQ discrepancy in the reading disabled population.'

[6] The Bangor Dyslexia test (T. R. Miles, 1983) can be cited as a simple and open test which does all that is necessary.

[7] C.f. Elaine Miles (Snowling and Thomson, 1991, p. 202) 'Finally, dividing dyslexics into groups by such artificial distinctions as we have found visual/auditory dyslexia to be leads to equally contrived artificial distinctions in teaching, instead of efforts being concentrated on those aspects of the written language which this particular child lacks, at the level he or she has reached.'

Chapter 2
The nature of
dyslexia

'. . . to an astonishing degree the components of communication can be
autonomous in the organisation and function of the brain.'

John Money (1962) *Reading Disability: progress
and research needs in dyslexia* (p. 14)

Introduction

Our discussion so far has aimed to demonstrate the presence of a
'dyslexia-shaped hole' in those explanations of illiteracy/subliteracy
which rely on what we have called 'visible causation'. We shall now
provide a more positive and substantial account, in the process
developing our view of dyslexia as a *language-related disability*. We
begin with a short account of the histories of four dyslexics whose
cases are either part of the documented history of dyslexia or else
well known to us personally. Anonymity, in one case at least, is rather
impossible, but we shall give all our subjects single letter surnames
for the sake of uniformity.

First case history: Mr W[1]

An extremely intelligent man of 68 suddenly discovers that he can no
longer read a single word or identify a single letter by name. He can
write words correctly but not read them back. Arabic numerals
present no difficulty. Having been a skilled musician, he is now quite
unable to comprehend musical notation but he can still write a scale
or particular notes to command.

For the remaining four years of his life he continues actively and
very successfully in business, plays cards skilfully, continues to write,
learns and performs new music by ear. After his death a post-mortem
examination is carried out by a distinguished neuro-anatomist, who

finds lesions (localised damage) in the left cerebral hemisphere (left side of the brain). In this patient, the lesions that caused the disability will have been the result of a blood clot leading to a stroke (cerebral thrombosis), a common cause of brain damage in later life. (Other causes of brain damage are: head injuries, oxygen deprivation and surgical procedures designed to relieve other conditions.) Symptoms like those of Mr W, have been repeatedly confirmed since, as has the link between damage affecting certain parts of the brain and impairment of language function, both spoken and written.

Mr W's dyslexia was *traumatic* – the result of a particular episode, in this case a stroke – and also highly *specific* in that it obliterated reading without affecting speech or general ability and with only a slight effect on writing. In technical terms, this was a case of *alexia* (loss of reading) without *agraphia* (loss of writing).

Second case history: Dr X

Dr X is a fellow of a Cambridge college working in the area of parasitology, and has been responsible for a large number of publications and research contributions. His father wished him to leave school at the age of 14 on the grounds that his severely retarded reading ruled out any possibility of a professional career. He still has difficulty with spelling, which he allows for by leaving gaps in words that seem difficult in the first draft so that he or his secretary can check them later. Telephone numbers are also a problem. It has seemed to him that his difficulties are bound up with problems of sequential ordering. He considers that the following expedients were helpful to him in overcoming his disability; a refusal to accept that spelling 'mattered', the ability to find alternative strategies (like memorising a page that was being read round the class), concentration on activities at which he could excel. In general, dyslexia has seemed to matter most at the beginning of the educational process and to become progressively less important.

Third case history: Miss Y[2]

Miss Y remembers at an early age frequently overhearing the word 'retarded' and wondering what it meant. Learning to read was difficult to impossible: 'Somehow the letters we put together never made me think of a word. They didn't make me think of anything.' She compensated for severe literacy problems by developing physical skills; '. . . my mother insisted on giving me dancing lessons every day of my life from the age of three onwards, thus helping to train my brain through movement, giving me good physical co-ordination, eliminating clumsiness and awkwardness, laying the foundations of hope.' Despite a formidable problem with auditions, which generally involve reading from a script, Miss Y has established herself as a highly successful actress on stage, screen and television. Now at the height of her career she notices the following persistent dyslexic symptoms:

> 'An average script takes the actor one-and-a-half to three hours to read; the same script takes me from three to five hours.' Almost completely unable to use a tele-prompter. Once discovered that she was driving about Los Angeles on the wrong side of the road. 'I wrote a great "R" on my right palm and an "L" on my left.'

> Day-to-day problems have included difficulty with

> > reading to children in bed
> > using recipes (allows three to four hours to prepare a meal that should take three-quarters of an hour)
> > helping with homework
> > reading letters over breakfast
> > checking change
> > filling in form for child allowance
> > reading label on medicine bottle
> > following 'A–Z' street maps
> > writing cheques so that words and figures correspond
> > retaining a telephone number long enough to dial.

Miss Y's success in overcoming a severe dyslexia can be attributed to a supportive environment in childhood ('I was protected and encouraged') coupled with talent and determination.

Fourth case history: John B[3]

At the time of writing, John B was working for O-levels in top stream for mathematics, geography, chemistry, physics, biology, technical drawing and rural studies. He had made little or no progress in reading at the age of seven, when he was assessed, first by a local authority psychologist and later by a private psychologist who reported an IQ of 125 (Wechsler Intelligence Test) and a 'severe degree of specific dyslexia' coupled with a weak span of auditory attention. Remediation has continued up to the present and has allowed the opportunity for frequent discussions with John's parents.

Progress was satisfactory but his tutor felt that it rested on a prodigious and sustained daily effort both at special tuition and at school.

Even now, on a bad day, John can regress to an 8-year-old reading level, unable to read a word like *train*.

The tutor employed a structured phonic programme combined with a multi-sensory teaching method. John's father, a driver/inspector for the local bus company, and his mother saw to it that his condition was recognised and treated in time and the favourable outcome is largely attributable to them and to his own high level of motivation.

The Studies Compared

These short studies are quite illuminating in their similarities and in their differences; all four subjects suffering from an impairment or deficit in *visual language function*, which left spoken language unaffected. We consider some points of comparison in the next sections.

Traumatic Dyslexia

Mr W's impairment was the most specific, since it affected reading but not writing/spelling or numbers. He also differs from the other subjects in that his dyslexia was *traumatic* (the result of injury or illness) while theirs was *developmental* (the symptoms are not associated with injury or illness; they make themselves apparent in the course of childhood development and seem to arise within it). This leads to the further difference that Mr W's trauma left visible traces on the brain in the form of lesions which were readily identifiable at autopsy whereas the brains of Dr X, Miss Y and John B, which happily are not available for dissection, would probably look no different from anyone else's.[4]

Despite these differences, Mr W's *traumatic* dyslexia is helpful to us in our approach to *developmental* dyslexia since his case (and the innumerable comparable cases which have been studied and documented since) allows us to conclude that dyslexia is *possible*. Mr W's case does *not* tell us that developmental dyslexias like those of Dr X, Miss Y and John B are caused by damage to, or abnormal development of, the cellular structure of the brain, but it *does* tell us that reading skills are built into the organisation and function of the brain in such way that they *can* be specifically affected.[5] And, in this context, it is not unreasonable to say that what can be disrupted traumatically can, in principle, be disrupted developmentally.

Of course, a demonstration that the brains of developmental dyslexics *did* show visible abnormalities would have the convenient result of finally disposing of any further controversy about the existence of dyslexia. However, the contrary view (that the brains of dyslexics do not bear superficial or microscopic signs of abnormality) can be accepted without any adverse effect on our argument since there are several more or less serious conditions which are generally agreed to result from a disturbance of brain function but which leave no visible traces in brain-tissue structure. Examples of such conditions are epilepsy, Down's syndrome, autism, colour-blindness and stuttering.

In order to understand how this is possible, it is necessary to appreciate that the human brain is a vastly complex organisation in which more than 15 000 million neurones are intricately linked with one another. At our current stage of knowledge and with available instrumentation, we have no way of even describing a particular disposition of neuronal circuitry, let alone identifying it as normal or abnormal. There is thus no reason to quarrel with the assertion that 'Dyslexia ... may involve no apparent tissue damage and yet result from developmental neurological difficulty of a functional nature' (Frank Vellutino in Benton and Pearl, 1978, p. 65.)

Effects of Brain Trauma

It may be of interest at this point to list some of the elements of language function that are known to have been disrupted by injury, damage or disease affecting the brain. In their variety and specificity they provide striking confirmation for the claim that '... to an astonishing degree, the components of communication can be autonomous [separate and independent] in the organisation and function of the brain' (John Money, *Reading Disability: progress and reseach needs in dyslexia*).

It will be noticed that some disruptions affect speech (audible language) and some affect reading/writing (visual language).

Conditions known to have resulted from focal lesions affecting the language centres of the left hemisphere

The patient may be affected in any of the following ways:

1   *Cannot speak,* but intelligence, hearing, silent reading and writing are unimpaired. The patient knows the words he wants to say but cannot get them out.
2   *Cannot read,* although vision is perfect and the patient may be able to spell and even write (but not read back what he has written).

3   *Cannot understand speech.* The patient hears perfectly, but reports
        (after recovery) that his own language sounded like a foreign
        tongue (*Encyclopaedia Britannica*, 15th Edition, Volume 17, p. 489).
4   *Cannot write rationally*, although his hand is able to grasp the pen.
5   *Cannot understand specific areas of language;* for instance, passive
        construction–the patient is able to interpret complicated and
        technical sentences, but on hearing the sentence 'the man was
        eaten by the tiger' is unable to say whether it was the man or
        the tiger who survived the encounter.
6   Can repeat what he has heard but *without understanding.*
7   *Can read ordinary words but not nonsense* words like *bont, kerg.*
8   Can read *some kinds of words* more easily than others (e.g.
        concrete nouns such as *table* more easily than 'grammatical'
        words like *but).*
9   Makes *semantic errors* e.g. *table* read as *chair.*
10   Can understand printed words, if at all, only on the basis of a
        laborious and often erroneous application of *'phonic' reading
        strategy.* (see N.C. Ellis and T.R Miles in Pavlidis and Miles,
        1981, p. 207).

Readers who work with dyslexic children may notice some parallels
between the traumatic symptoms noted above and certain developmental anomalies which they encounter regularly in practice. For
instance, it is not uncommon to find children who have been diagnosed as dyslexic and who

•   can write an accurate representation of a printed sentence but
        have great difficulty in reading it back (reminiscent of 2
        above);
•   seem to recognise a word as part of a general category without
        relating it to its sound – ladder is read as steps; hut as shed.
        (reminiscent of 9 above).

    The last category of traumatic impairment (10 above) sounds like
a description of standard developmental dyslexia
    Our brief discussion of traumatic dyslexia has raised a number of
relevant points:

1.   Since a whole range of language problems can be induced by
        brain traumata (including one that rather resembles 'ordinary
        dyslexia'), it is theoretically possible that a developmental
        disorder of neural function could have an effect limited to one
        or more aspects of language, including visual language.

2. While a developmental dyslexia – that is, one not caused by injury or disease but constitutional in origin – *might* be associated with visible traces in the cellular structure of the brain, it is also possible for a developmental disorder to affect neural function in a dramatic fashion *without* leaving any traces detectable with presently available techniques.

3. Language function has been shown to be controlled in most people by localised areas within the cellular structure of the brain (normally within the left hemisphere), within which there appear to be segments that relate particularly to *visual language*. The evidence for these statements is that damage to these areas has consistently been found to affect language function in certain ways. As one might expect, the areas are noticeably more developed anatomically in man than in other animals and this is observable even in the unborn foetus.[6] It appears therefore that the areas do not develop as a result of the individual's use of language, but rather that they have become specialised in the course of human evolution and now condition the emergence of language in the individual. However

4. Mysteriously, and rather contradictorily, language can still appear even when the left side of the brain is removed. If this is done in babyhood (as sometimes occurs when there is an invasive tumour) language develops quite normally.

We can now leave the case of Mr W and turn to the cases of *developmental* dyslexia.

Developmental Dyslexia: Some Preliminary Considerations

It may be appropriate at this point to say something about case studies in general. These are sometimes presented rather apologetically as though their narrative quality detracted in some way from their value as scientific evidence. It has been stated, for instance, that 'from their very nature clinical observations are less "secure" than the results of systematic experimentation.' This seems to put the case too strongly; we consider that case studies and experiments can both contribute to the advancement of knowledge and that the one is as valid as the other. Even the most sophisticated and elaborate experiments are certainly not immune from the effects of unconscious bias – for instance, some findings may be emphasised at the expense of others – and the very complexity of the project may make such bias more difficult to detect. Also, there may be a tendency to accord respect to experimental work for its own sake, even when the effect on scientific advance has been rather meagre. Case studies, in contrast, provide very direct, if selective, insights into the problem being studied. The subjects of our histories are not figments, or unique creatures (except in the sense that we all are), or accomplices, but human beings whose lives have been powerfully affected by the problems that they have perceived and described. It is certainly not in their interests to exaggerate their handicap – quite the contrary – but they have been prepared to place their experience at the disposal of other people who have encountered or may encounter similar difficulties. We can now consider what light their cases throw on the condition that we are calling developmental dyslexia.

First, the similarity of their symptoms provides some support for the hypothesis that is permitted by cases like that of Mr W. If there is a developmental anomaly of brain function that mimics some of the traumatic anomalies discussed above, then one would expect that sufferers from this anomaly would exhibit similar clusters of symptoms – in clinical language, a syndrome. This expectation is satisfied in the cases we have selected. Among several similarities we can note:

1.   The *severity* of the condition. In all cases we seem to encounter, not so much slow or delayed progress in reading, as a bar to any progress at all. '. . . prognosis for dyslexia, given no specialist intervention is, therefore, very poor' (Val Muter (1982) 'The relationship between definitions and assessment in dyslexia,' *Dyslexia Review*, Vol 5, No. 1).

2.   The *persistence* of the condition. Dr X and Miss Y bear witness, in adulthood, to a problem that has been overcome but certainly not cured, despite strong incentives and admirable personal qualities. It is inconceivable that a condition that was educational in origin (caused perhaps by difficulties in schooling), or familial (the result of some kind of parental fixation), could be so resistant. Both these characteristics are what one would expect to find in a constitutional condition. They are not what would be expected in slow reading caused by general backwardness which, in any case, as we have already noted, does not of itself inhibit the acquisition of literacy. Many children with Down's syndrome and more severe conditions successfully learn to read.

Second, the outlook. In different ways, each of our subjects provides much encouragement for dyslexics. Dr X and Miss Y have built successful careers despite their past and present disabilities, and built them, moreover, in professions which set a premium on sophisticated literacy. The case of John B shows similar problems being countered by appropriate educational methods in the context of a supportive home and school environment.

In the next section, we begin to give a reasoned account of the approaches likely to be most effective in helping other dyslexics towards their final objective of overcoming not the disability itself, but its most harmful consequences.

Notes

[1]   Dejerine's account of this case is summarised by Norman Geschwind in Money, J. (Ed.) 1962, *Reading Disability: progress and research needs in dyslexia*, p.117

[2]   From *Susan's Story* by Susan Hampshire. Sidgwick and Jackson, 1981.

[3]   A more detailed version of this case study will be found on p. 82

[4]   There are two cases reported in the literature of dyslexics who were found on autopsy to have congenital cerebral malformations. However, both subjects had been abnormal in ways that went beyond dyslexia. The search for other instances continues. See R.I. Masland in Pavlidis and Miles (1981).

[5]   Shankweiler and Crain (1986) take as given the view of the human language apparatus as a biologically coherent or 'evolved' system 'distinguished from other parts of the cognitive apparatus by special brain structures and other anatomical specialisations'.

[6]   'This concentration of language function in the left side of the brain is reflected in significant asymmetries of brain structures . . . demonstrable even in the unborn child' (Pavlidis and Miles, 1981, p. 39).

Chapter 3
Developmental dyslexia: cause and effect

'... all those muddled ideas of multiple aetiology ...'

J. Macdonald Critchley (1970) *The Dyslexic Child*, p. xii.

Introduction

Parents and teachers who work with dyslexic children are governed by two sets of constraints. In the first place they must be responsive to the personal and intellectual problems that are specific to dyslexia. Second, they are answerable to general principles of good teaching which apply in all subjects and at all levels (Figure 7). Pre-eminent among these is the principle that teaching will be easiest and most effective when it is seen to grow out of a coherent system of ideas – more concisely: 'You can't teach what you don't know' (the title of a paper by Dr Joyce Morris, UKRA, 1962). It follows that the point of departure for *Dealing with Dyslexia* must be a clear mental appreciation of its underlying structure. In this section, we shall present some ideas which have implications for teachers of dyslexics and show how they have been related to research. We shall also lay the foundations of a sensible, useful and believable theory of dyslexia.

In this section especially we shall be drawing on review material and discussion contained in two publications which have been influential in developing our thinking about dyslexia: *Dyslexia: theory and research* by Frank Vellutino (MIT Press, 1979) and *A Lexical Encoding Deficiency* (two papers by N.C. Ellis and T.R. Miles[1]) We find ourselves in general agreement with the conclusions reached by these writers, which take shape for us in the proposition, now accepted by the majority of workers in the field, that dyslexia is what it appears to be – an impairment of *language*, the neural anomaly

referred to above making itself manifest through the processes that
underlie writing, reading and the production of speech. It follows
that effective remediation will demand, from teachers and all others
concerned with education, close attention to, and a good understanding of, these linguistic processes.

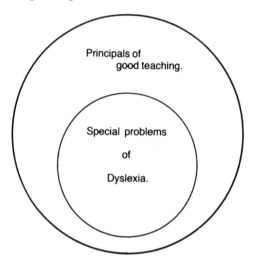

Figure 7. Constraints on teachers and parents of Dyslexics.

Inaccessibility

All attempts to investigate mental processes are faced with a problem of *inaccessibility*, since the cerebral events that produce the various activities of mental life are both physically and conceptually
beyond the present reach of scientific investigation. Accordingly,
since we cannot hope to arrive at the underlying structure of
dyslexia by direct observation of the functioning brain, it becomes
necessary to adopt a more indirect approach in which the signs and
symptoms of dyslexia, which *are* available for study, form the basis
for deductions about the nature and treatment of the underlying
condition. (Cognitive psychology and behavioural psychology both
take this as their point of departure, but from there on their paths
diverge. We shall be referring to some of the techniques and conclusions of *behavioural* and *developmental* psychology). We begin our treatment by listing:

The signs and symptoms of developmental dyslexia

The dyslexic has unusual difficulty with:

reading: progress is late and slow, seems to lack mental support, each attempt is a fresh start.

spelling: even more resistant than reading, the kinds of mistake are distinctive – often seem unrelated to the standard orthography, sometimes 'phonetic' and sometimes not.

writing: it is not so much the physical act of writing that is affected (though that may be troublesome), but letters may be reversed (<d> becomes <b>) and so may words (<was> becomes <saw>) and letters within words (<lion> becomes <loin>). It seems that the three threads of writing itself, letter formation and spelling are entangled here. The problems mentioned under this head are common to all beginning readers/writers, but are far more severe and resistant with dyslexics.

speech: occasionally. Generally, speech is not affected, but dyslexics are sometimes late in developing it.

digits and numbers: forming and orienting digits may be a difficulty but the problem is more one of 'spelling', getting and retaining numbers in correct sequence.

sequencing: noticeable with numbers, but may make itself apparent with letters, words or even objects; note that sequence may take two forms – spatial (in space), when letters or objects have to be *arranged* in a certain order, and temporal (in time), when words have to be *said* (one after another) in a certain order. The first characterises written, and the second, spoken language. The logical sequencing of ideas also presents difficulties for some older children.

memory: dyslexics are often reported to have difficulty in remembering, which may show itself in recalling sentences or numbers or in remembering errands or other instructions. The most conspicuous difficulty arises with reading/spelling; a word that was mastered on Monday is lost again on Tuesday.

orientation: confusion between left and right, which occurs in all young children is much more persistent in dyslexics. Left and right are difficult both as concepts and as guides to action in a particular situation – the dyslexic turns right when he or she should turn left. Possibly as a consequence of

	this difficulty dyslexics are sometimes accused of *clumsiness*.
specific tasks:	dyslexics are found to have difficulty with a number of tasks, which may or may not be linked to the above, for instance: colour naming, reading the time, learning and repeating months of the year and multiplication tables, repeating back a long word, dressing, tying shoelaces, finding their way about school.

Research

'Positive associations of a modest degree have been found between reading retardation and deviant performance on a variety of tasks making demands on perceptual, linguistic, sequencing and intersensory integrative abilities. *In truth it would be difficult to find a task on which reading-disabled children have not been reported to be deficient.* At the same time, failure to find differences between good and poor readers has also been reported with respect to these performances.' (Arthur Benton, in Benton and Pearl, 1978, p. 468 (our emphasis))

Over the years, a large body of research has grown up around the signs and symptoms listed above, largely within the discipline of behavioural psychology. Its objectives have not always been clearly defined, but, essentially, there has been the attempt to probe the underlying causes of dyslexia *by reasoning backwards from the surface symptoms.* Generally, the following procedures have been employed:

The researcher

1. Contemplates the symptoms of dyslexia.
2. Speculates about possible causal factors – for instance he or she might decide that the difficulties experienced by the dyslexic were due to a particular and specific weakness of visual memory.
3. Establishes to his/her own satisfaction that (in this case) visual memory has 'thing status' in the neural apparatus.
4. Devises a task which tests the supposed weakness and
5. Administers it to a group of dyslexics and to a control group of normal readers. (The problems involved in defining a research population for the study of dyslexia are analysed in Vellutino (1979), Chapter 2.)

If there is a significant difference between the performances of the two groups (if, for instance, the dyslexics turn out to have a significantly worse visual memory than the members of the control group), then the researcher will take this as evidence that a distinguishing and perhaps crucial characteristic of dyslexia has been identified; probably he/she will go on to propose a programme of remediation aimed at the presumed deficiency. Figure 8, column B, contains a fairly comprehensive list of the defects that have been blamed for failure in reading.

A	B
Signs and symptoms – the dyslexia syndrome	Possible causal factors in no particular order*
Persistent difficulty with reading – silent and loud writing – letters and digits reversed or disordered spelling orientation memory	The dyslexic has been accused of deficiencies in or disorders of short-term memory 'serial order recall' 'spatial/directional sense' 'sequential ordering' orientation 'sense of symmetry'
Exceptional difficulty with reading the time repeating months of the year multiplication tables long words colour naming	'intersensory integration' maturation (delayed) perceptuo-motor function (scanning eye movements) perception (visual/auditory) muscular co-ordination language function

Figure 8: Multiplicity: a summary of the *effects* (column A) and proposed *causes* (column B) of dyslexia.

* With regard to the items in column B, it must be emphasised, first, that they are not in any particular order relative to the items in column A; second, that they are put in mainly for reference. Apart from *language function*, they will not be considered further in this book. Vellutino (1979) contains a full discussion.

Before going on to discuss this type of research, it may be helpful to provide an example.

'A further study of some cognitive and other disabilities in backward readers of average non-verbal reasoning scores' (Lovell, Gray and Oliver, 1964). In this experiment, a group of 'backward' and a group of 'non-backward' readers, aged 14–15 years, were compared in the task of *reproducing a piece of text* (10 sentences).

Two methods of reproduction were tested:

1.   The subjects copied a *visually displayed* text.
2.   The text was not displayed but the subjects wrote down the sentences from dictation.

It appeared that when the text was *displayed and copied*, there was no significant difference between the performance of the two groups, but when the text was *dictated and not displayed*, the group of poor readers made significantly more mistakes than the group of normal readers.

These results could be interpreted in two ways:

1.   Poor readers can see as well as good readers, but their hearing is defective. This idea can be tested by giving all the subjects an audiometric examination. Supposing this theory to have been disproved, we can turn to the second interpretation;
2.   The difference in performance reflects a *linguistic difference* between the two tasks, the second being more complex. The copying task demanded only a *visual* skill, the ability to perceive and reproduce shapes. Poor readers can do this as well as normal readers. The dictation task demanded *linguistic* skills; the message was received in one code (heard as audible language) and had to be decoded (understood) in that mode; then it had to be recoded into another mode (written as visual language). Poor readers find this more difficult than normal readers do, and therefore they make more mistakes.

The results supported the second hypothesis

Problems with behavioural research

The experiment described above indicates that behavioural research provides an interesting and necessary technique for getting at the underlying causal structure of dyslexia by probing beneath its superficial symptoms. Perhaps it is the most effective method available to us at present. Nevertheless its contribution has been weakened by two serious defects. The first is

Multiplicity (Figure 8)

While researchers have shown themselves to be very effective at identifying and testing possible causal factors, they have been much less effective at analysing the results in a critical way, discarding the less credible and extracting a coherent pattern from what remains. Instead, the conclusions thrown up by successive waves of experimentation have been allowed to *accumulate* to the point where they now constitute a formidable obstacle both to a clear view of the subject and to effective action. The array of semi-contradictory causes that continues to be invoked to explain symptoms and justify treatments is totally confusing for the practitioner and seriously weakens the credibility of dyslexia as an objectifiably valid condition.

Attempts to remedy the situation by proposing that dyslexia might have *numerous causes* (Figure 9) or that there might be *several different dyslexias*[2] (one to suit each favoured theory of causation) (Figure 10) do not improve matters.

We regard dyslexia as a unitary condition with a single cause. (Figure 11 below.)

The second defect of behavioural research arises from its inability to come to grips with the fundamental nature of the topic. Instead of recognising reading and writing as unique activities flowing from a unique human capability, behavioural research has tended to treat them as though they were no different from other activities requiring precise visual and muscular control. Consequently, its findings have often failed to capture the essence of the subject being studied.

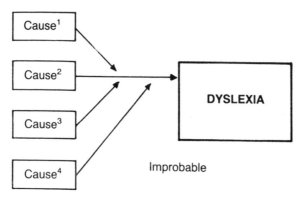

Figure 9. Multiple causes converge to produce a single complex condition.

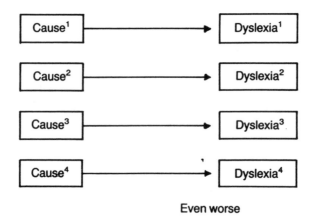

Figure 10. Multiple Dyslexias

Michael Stubbs remarks that: 'This lacuna is part of a more general failure, in much of the experimental psychological literature, to regard reading and writing as *linguistic* processes. Reading has often been seen predominantly as a matter of visual processing, involving characteristic eye movements, perceptual span, word gestalts and so on. As a result it has often been ignored that what people read is linguistically organised and meaningfully structured' (Stubbs, 1980, p. 5) In brief, the research effort has partly failed in its objectives because researchers have tended not to have, or not to use, the insights provided by the science of linguistics.[3]

The logical structure of dyslexia

Figure 11 expresses our conviction that dyslexia arises out of a single cause which can only be tackled effectively by those who recognise its essentially and intrinsically linguistic character.[4] The diagram claims further that the factors in column II, which have all, at one time or another, been thought of as causal, are not causes at all, but 'side-effects' or 'consequences' of the primary cause. One could say that the primary linguistic cause operates in ways that admit of misinterpretation and that the 'false causes' are various different ways of misinterpreting it.

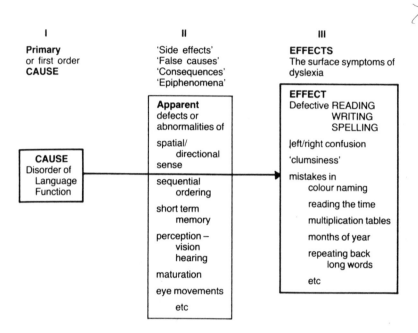

Figure 11. The logical structure of dyslexia. An underlying disorder of *language function* accounts for all the signs and symptoms of dyslexia. The operation of this cause sets up a number of consequential effects which may be mistakenly thought of as causal.

Notes

[1]   In Pavlidis and Miles (1981).

[2]   The work of Elena Boder (e.g. Boder, 1971) is sometimes cited in support of the idea of differentiated dyslexias. However, her identification of three subtypes seems to rest on the questionable assumption that rapid word recognition (i.e. within 2 seconds) must occur without the intervention of any linguistic process. See remarks by Stubbs (1980) p. 32.

[3]   The situation has improved very considerably in this respect since the appearance of the first edition of *Dealing with Dyslexia* (see introduction, p.xv).

[4]   C.f. Elaine Miles (Snowling and Thomson, 1991, p. 202).

Chapter 4
Language

Introduction

Since the view of dyslexia that we are now developing assigns to *language* the role of primary determinant cause, it becomes necessary at this point to say what language is and then go on to show how its disruption can bring about the symptomatic behaviours associated with dyslexia. We should also indicate what implications this view carries for teachers, parents and others who wish to give practical help to dyslexics. These topics are dealt with in the remainder of Book One.

Chapter 4 gives an extended account of *language*; Chapter 5 shows how a disruption of language could be responsible for the signs and symptoms associated with dyslexia; Chapter 6 describes how insights from *linguistics* can contribute to the teaching of dyslexic children and adults.

On Language

Language is the expression of a *uniquely human attribute* not possessed by any other creature. It operates in human beings by virtue of a genetic programme comparable to those that control other complex human and animal behaviours: for instance, web-making in spiders; nest-building in birds. Dyslexia is a minor malfunction in this programme. Language exists in three forms (Figure 12).

1 Inside one's head as 'knowledge of language'

The language faculty is present and functioning in humans at all times whether they are engaging in language behaviour or not. Since the faculty is genetically conditioned, it is present even in babies who have not yet developed speech.

(The following discussion derives partly from Eric Lenneberg (1967) *The Biological Foundations of Language*, New York: Wiley.)

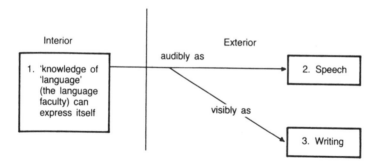

Figure 12. The three faces of language

It is held by some that language is not a separate and isolatable human attribute, but is merely a natural outcome of the high intelligence possessed by the human species. If this were the case, it could not be specifically impaired. However, the following evidence suggests that there is, in fact, a separate and uniquely human 'faculty of language'.

a. Language can be disrupted traumatically, therefore there must be a sense in which it is distinguishable in neural function and hence available to be disrupted (see introduction, p. xii). Dramatic disturbance of the language faculty can occur, as with Mr W, without affecting general intelligence to any appreciable extent.

b. Language is species specific. If language were an outgrowth of general mental capacity, one would expect that all 'higher animals' would possess it in a degree proportional to their intelligence. This is self-evidently not the case, although they have developed other, and equally remarkable, attributes. In this connection, one should perhaps mention the various projects aimed at persuading chimpanzees to interact linguistically. These experiments have not been successful.

c. Language is species uniform. All human beings and all human societies employ languages that are based on similar principles and are of equal complexity. There are no 'primitive languages'. This is what one would expect, given that language grows out of a universal, 'built-in' human attribute.

d. Language is independent of intelligence. If language were a function of general intelligence, one would expect it to vary smoothly with the intelligence of the user, with major differences at the two ends of the normal range. Language is, in fact, operated identically by humans at all levels of intelligence, with only minor and superficial variation. Only profound mental retardation inhibits language.

e. Spoken language does not have to be taught. If language were not an 'innate faculty', it would have to be learned from scratch by each individual human being. However, it is far too complex to be mastered like this in early childhood without concentrated and skilful instruction. On the contrary, it emerges spontaneously in the individual whether he or she receives instruction or not. Short of prolonged and total isolation, it is impossible to prevent small children from learning to speak.

f. It is now well established that small children everywhere develop the different stages of language *at much the same ages and in the same order.* This is consistent with the existence of an inbuilt language faculty and there is no way that it could occur otherwise without a universally imposed, stereotyped, uniform and systematic teaching programme, which, of course, does not exist.

2 'Knowledge-of-language' is expressed audibly, as speech

3 'Knowledge-of-language' is expressed visibly, as writing

Speech

Language function in all three aspects depends on the human ability to make a link between

> *a.* the objects and events which make up the world of human experience and
>
> *b.* a system of *arbitrary symbols* (words).

In *speech* these symbols take the form of airborne sound vibrations which humans have learned to control and interpret with great skill. The *arbitrariness* of the symbols allows them to become the elements of an infinitely rapid and expressive system of communication and is thus their most important characteristic.

Arbitrariness of linguistic symbols

It is accurate, although oversimple, to say that human language is essentially a device for associating *things* with *sounds.* Figure 13 (based on *The Meaning of Meaning* by C.K. Ogden and I.A. Richards, 1923, p. 11) shows how a *thing*

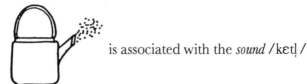

is associated with the *sound* /ketl/

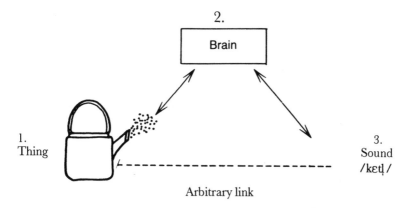

Figure 13. The anatomy of a word

The link between object and sound is *arbitrary* (dotted line) and dependent on a linguistic association via the brain (solid arrows). All three elements are needed to create a *word*. (Symbols of the International Phonetic Alphabet are used here between obliques to indicate that we are referring to *sounds* and not to *letters*. A complete list of phonemic symbols is printed in Appendix C.)

The connection between  and **/ketl̩/** is a purely linguistic association which takes place only within language. The two are linked because the English language has decreed that they shall be linked *and for no other reason*. There is nothing intrinsic to the sound /ketl̩/ which belongs to a metallic water heater and nothing about a metallic water heater which suggests the sound /ketl̩/ or indeed any sound, except perhaps a prolonged hissing bubbling noise. The dotted line between

and /ketl̩/

in Figure 13 indicates the artificial and indirect nature of the relationship between them, while the solid arrows indicate the 'real' link via the human brain, which contains in some form a register of cultural decisions about *meanings*. Our ability to make arbitrary links of this kind is part of our inherited genetic endowment, while the actual links that we do make come to us as part of our learned cultural endowment. *Nature* and *nurture* collaborate in the linguistic process whereby sounds become the words of a language.

Because the relation between words and things is arbitrary, it follows that a language is free within limits to attach *any* sound to *any* thing, the main restriction being that too many meanings should not be assigned to the same sound. Apart from this limitation, one sound is as good as another for the purpose, and a 'universal' object like *pebble* will have been represented by thousands of *different* sounds in the past and present languages of the human world. This fact is sufficient to demonstrate the essentially arbitrary basis of human language.

Disruption of Audible Language Function

It may be conjectured that the arbitrariness of the link between sound and object renders it particularly vulnerable to disruption.

It can be disrupted *traumatically*, as we saw on p. 17–18, Case 3. These symptoms (cannot understand speech, the patient hears perfectly but reports, after recovery, that his own language sounded like a foreign tongue) must be those of a person who has suffered a traumatic severance of the linkage shown in Figure 13; no other explanation could account for the ability to hear one's own language without understanding it.

It is at least plausible that the puzzling condition known as autism represents a *developmental* disruption of audible language function.

Autism

The first published description of the symptoms of autism (1943) emphasised disturbances in the development of speech and language and it is now widely recognised that disturbances of language and language development are central features in early infantile autism. The characteristic signs (lack of speech, profound withdrawal, highly stereotyped or ritualistic behaviour) begin to manifest themselves very early in life and are consistent with language impairment: 'This is not to say that language impairment need be the only handicap of autistic children... Nevertheless it is reasonable to enquire whether the critical signs of autism, i.e. those signs which are common to *all* autistic children, may not be a manifestation of an *underlying impairment of language function* [our emphasis]. There is the distinct possibility that such language impairment is a necessary and sufficient proximate cause of infantile autism' (from Churchhill, *The Language of Autistic Children*, 1978, p. 7).

Michael Rutter offers the following general summary of the direction of research in autism: 'Perhaps the most striking shift of all has been the move from seeing autism as a condition involving social and emotional *withdrawal* to a view of autism as a disorder of development involving severe *cognitive* defects which probably have their origin in some form of organic brain disfunction' (in *Autism, a reappraisal of concepts and treatment*, edited by M. Rutter and E. Schopler, 1978, p. 85).

Summary

Spoken language rests on the genetically conditioned ability to make symbolic connections between objects and sounds (audible language function); such connections are arbitrary and can be disrupted both traumatically and developmentally.

In our view, the problems associated with dyslexia arise from comparable difficulties over *written language* (visual language function).

Writing and Reading

Visual language follows exactly the same principle as audible language – it represents the objects of human experience by means of arbitrary symbols. However, the audible and the visual modes differ in three important ways.

Differences between Spoken and Writing Language

1. First, there is the obvious difference of *medium*; marks rather than sounds are used to make up the substance of the symbols. This feature gives to written language its prime virtue of *permanence* and no doubt explains why it was necessary to invent it.
2. Second, there is a less obvious difference of *level*. This can be explained quite simply by saying that while speech arises out of and interacts with *language*, writing arises out of an interaction with *speech* (Figure 14)[1].

The same idea is expressed in Figure 15, which is a developed version of Figure 13.

Pointed brackets around a word or symbol, <kettle>, mean that we are paying attention to it as a written (visible) object.

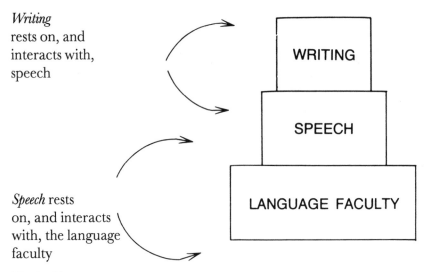

Writing rests on, and interacts with, speech

Speech rests on, and interacts with, the language faculty

Figure 14.

Obliques around a word or symbol mean that we are paying attention to it as a spoken (audible) object. Note also that
    <word> means 'written word'
    /word/ means 'spoken word'

We shall discuss the relationship between spoken and written

/kɛtl/ is an arbitrary representation of

<kettle> is an arbitrary representation of /kɛtl\

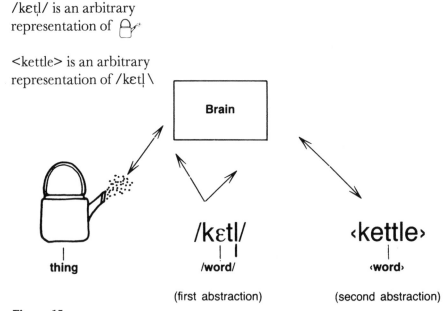

Figure 15.

language more fully in Book Three. The following points need to be made here;

a. <kettle> represents /ketl̩/ *step-by-step in segments*, that is to say the first or left-most bit of <kettle>, namely <k>, can be thought of as representing the 'first' sound of /ketl̩/ namely /k/, and so on.[2] The relationship is a notoriously elastic one, but it certainly exists and supplies the dominating logic of the alphabetic writing system.

b. <kettle> is *arbitrary*, just as /ketl̩/ is. There is positively nothing intrinsic to the *shape* <k> which belongs to the *sound* represented by /k/ (the sound of pent-up air being released from behind the tongue)

< Ӿ > or < ⤳ > would do just as well

and so would < ⊤⌐ >

or any other convenient mark.

Indeed, in a very real sense, <kettle> is more arbitrary than /ketl̩/ since it is a double arbitrariness at two removes – an abstraction from an abstraction.

<kettle> is an arbitrary representation of an arbitrary representation of

It appears, then, that the activity of reading/writing draws on the same innate resource as does the activity of speaking/understanding, but at a still more abstract and elaborate level. Perhaps that is why reading is more readily disrupted than speaking. It would be natural that a minor neural anomaly of language function should manifest itself in the more developed aspect, rather as a slight stiffness of the finger joints might affect piano playing but not the ability to saw timber. When the disability is severe enough to reach downwards towards the underlying faculty, as in autism, the consequences are unfortunately very serious.

3. The third and last distinction to be noted between audible and visual language function is a distinction of *development,* the written language representing a later stage of development than the spoken

language *both in the species and in the individual.* The emergence of spoken language probably coincided with, and to an unknown extent determined, the emergence of a distinct human *species*, just as the much later appearance of written language undoubtedly coincided with, and determined, the emergence of *human civilisation.* The first of these developments must have occurred at least 1 million years ago; the second can be dated with some precision to the third millennium before Christ – about 5000 years ago.

Spoken language is now programmed into the genetic make-up of the individual, emerging in babyhood with the same inevitability and the same orderliness that characterises the appearance of teeth. Teaching plays only a minor role in the acquisition of spoken language, which develops almost as early and as quickly without any instruction.

Written language, in contrast, was 'invented', has developed by cultural transition, is transmitted culturally and not genetically, appears at a later stage in the life of the individual and is dependent on teaching. Without special training it will not, except in rare cases, appear at all and it sometimes fails to develop even when teaching is available.

Disruption of visual language function

As with spoken, so with written language. Reading and writing can be impaired either traumatically ('brain damage') or developmentally ('dyslexia').

Notes

[1]   There is probably also some degree of interaction between written language and the language faculty; the simplification is acceptable in terms of the present discussion.

[2]   The nature of 'segmentation' is briefly considered in the introduction, p. xii. The statement here is perhaps too great a simplification since the sounds of a word are not, in fact, sequentially ordered. '... There are no acoustic boundaries between sounds in speech. Rather **sounds** are continuous and are folded into each other and co-articulated' (L.C. Ehri, citing Liberman et al., 1977, in Snowling and Thomson, 1991, page 68).

Chapter 5
Language and dyslexia

Introdution

The claim that dyslexia is caused by an impairment of language function is unsustainable unless it can be shown convincingly that the various signs and symptoms of dyslexia, which are listed on pp. 7–8, *could* be caused by a simple defect of language without the need to invoke failures of vision, memory, symmetry, co-ordination, orientation, maturation, integration and the rest.[1] We shall consider these various symptoms in turn.

Difficulties with Reading, Writing, Spelling, Digits. 'Anything Goes'

Evidently, this topic is central to our discussion and has to be interpreted in the light of what has gone before and especially in relation to our claim that the essence of language resides in a special human *aptitude for making connections* between the elements of experience on the one hand and a set of linguistic symbols on the other. These connections are governed by the law of *Anything Goes*. Within limits, *any* symbol, whether spoken or written will stand equally well for a particular object or event, as long as it is accepted by a community of language users. This peculiarity of language is advantageous since it places at our disposal an infinite repertoire of linguistic signs and sounds which can be used to mirror the equally vast range of human facts, objects and experiences. In this way, the sum total of human knowledge and experience can be matched to a functioning language system.

However, the advantage is conditional. It operates *only* by and through the human talent for creating and maintaining symbolic linkages and it is precisely this ability that seems to be selectively impaired in the dyslexic. For him or her, the law of 'anything goes' takes on a different and sadly ironic significance: there is, indeed, for the dyslexic, 'no reason' why a word should be represented by one row of symbols rather than another, or why the symbols themselves should 'demand' a particular orientation. The inbuilt link which, for the ordinary child, forms the starting-point for the discovery of written language, is defective in the dyslexic child – all the difficulties flow from that.

The abstractness of written language renders it particularly vulnerable to disruption. Not only does it represent 'an abstraction from an abstraction' but it is in itself highly arbitrary or conventional' in several distinct ways:

1. The shapes of the letters are themselves arbitrary or conventional:

for instance, <n, u, s, k> are used in the 'Western' orthography

but not

which, from an objective point of view, would do equally well.

2. The *relation* between letter shapes and 'their' sounds is arbitrary/conventional – there is no reason why the letter <e> should represent the sound /ɛ/ as in *bed* rather than the sounds /b/ or /ʊ/, which occur as the first two elements in *book*. (A full explanation of all the symbols and their relation to sounds/letters is given in Book Three.)

On the other hand, the relation between a letter and its *name* is *non*-arbitrary and helpful for teaching purposes because in almost every case the name provides a *bridge* between the symbol and the sound. For instance, the letter *name*

'B'   (=/bi/)

and the corresponding sound[2, 3]

/b (ə)/

are made with the same articulatory movement (compressed air released from behind closed lips).

In the same way the *continuant* in the name for

'M' (/ɛmmm.../)

enacts the equivalent speech sound.

The rule 'A' says 'a' "/eɪ sɛz æ/) encapsulates *both* the basic sounds associated with the symbol which is generally written as <ɑ> and printed as <a>. (See also Book Three, Chapter 1, notes 10 and 11.)

It seems reasonable that children should be informed of these regularities.

3. The *left-to-right* arrangement of letters and of written words to correspond with the order of the sounds is arbitrary and reversed in some writing systems – Arabic, Yiddish.

'Somehow the letters we put together never made me think of a word – they didn't make me think of anything.' (see p. 18)

Miss Y, like other dyslexics, has had to achieve by a painful and repetitive effort of reason the results which come naturally, unreflectingly and, as it were, instinctively, to the ordinary person. Yet, all too often, the teaching that dyslexics receive is based on assumptions derived from normal practice. In the light of the foregoing discussion, readers will probably have no difficulty in accepting that a comparatively mild dislocation of language could reasonably be expected to give rise to the severe and persistent problems with reading, writing and spelling, which form the 'major' symptoms of dyslexia.

The formation and arrangement of numbers could also be expected to give rise to difficulties, since the shapes of the 10 digits are conventional in just the same way that the 26 letters are, and their arrangement to form numbers is also governed by convention. The *names* of *digits*, unlike those of letters, are no help, since they say nothing at all about the function of the symbol that they represent. This may explain the common difficulty over recall of telephone numbers.

Orientation: Left and Right

In order to understand why orientation should present special problems for dyslexics and how these problems can originate in language difficulties, it will be necessary first to enquire how 'sense of direction' functions in the *normal* individual.

In the first place, we can assume that human beings occupy a 3-dimensional space and that the three dimensions, although mathematically alike, are perceived differently.

We shall consider each dimension in turn.

1. *Up and down*

The vertical dimension is 'given' and 'absolute' in a sense that does not apply to the other two, in fact it is given to us in three distinct ways:

first, it corresponds to *sky and earth* – it is given by our surroundings;

second, it corresponds to *head and foot*; it is given by human anatomy;

third, it corresponds to the directional pull of *gravity*; it is given by physical laws which have their physiological counterpart in the device, much like a spirit level, which is located in the middle ear and which at all times balances our posture against the vertical pull of gravitation.

'Up and down' then is, for all practical purposes, an absolute dimension, the same in all terrestrial times and places and therefore unlikely to give rise to uncertainty in dyslexics or anyone else.

2. *Backwards and forwards*, by contrast, is not an absolute dimension: it shifts from moment to moment according to our location. Nor is it given by our surroundings or by a natural law. It is therefore less stable than 'up and down' but it works sufficiently well because it corresponds to the basic structure of human anatomy. 'Forward' is the side of the body where the face is positioned along with other prominent features; it is the direction in which we most naturally look and point. 'Backwards' is the opposite direction. the direction of our 'back'. Although 'backwards and forwards' change from moment to moment as we shift our position, still at any particular instant we have no difficulty in pointing 'forward'.

3. *Left and right*

The third dimension is a very different affair from the other two. Not only does it shift from moment to moment like 'forwards and backwards' but it is based on co-ordinates that are not 'given' in any way – by our surroundings, by a natural law or even by anatomical structure – but are fixed by arbitrary convention. It is true that the right and left *hands* which we use as a point of reference for this dimension are mirror images of one another and therefore not interchangeable, but this is a matter of subtle mathematics and not of human perception. Anatomically, they are indistinguishable. (See also Martin

Gardner, *The Ambidextrous Universe*, Pelican, 1970.)

So how do we tell left from right?

In order to understand the answer to this question, we must distance ourselves from human preconceived ideas to the point where we are able to recognise that our left and right hands are different only because we *call them by different names;* each carries an invisible linguistic label.[4] This raises a further question, namely 'How do we know which hand to *call* right or left?' The answer to that question lies in a fact not of human anatomy but of human *function*: a working majority of human beings, probably about 75%, are 'left-brained' and therefore right-handed; most people, including dyslexics, use the same hand for holding pens, throwing spears and shaking hands. The dextrals, being in a comfortable, though by no means overwhelming majority have been able to win the day ('There is no disagreement about the right-handedness of all societies since the beginning of recorded history' (Gardner, 1970)); but the adoption of a right over left preference was probably not carried through unopposed since it has had to be bolstered up by resort to all kinds of moral and religious sanctions which are often to be found embedded in language. So we find the word 'right' associated with what is *good* ('right and proper') and *skilful* ('dextrous' from Latin 'dexter'), while left has been associated with what is *awkward* (French 'gauche') and *suspect* (Latin 'sinister'). Parallel examples can be provided from other cultures.

Once left and right have been established, the 3-dimensional grid falls into place too and human beings then have a mechanism for locating themselves spatially. Notice, however, that all three co-ordinates must be in place and in full working order before the system can function. Therefore our ability to locate ourselves and to convey a location to others rests in the last resort on language. A weakness in this area will be peculiarly undermining.

The points of the compass

The points of the compass are an extension of the 3-dimensional grid to cover the surface of the globe. As long as everyone is 'the same way up' (no problem) and faces in the same direction (north), then north will be forwards, south will be backwards and east and west will be *right* and *left* under a different name. The points of the compass, in other words, also depend on a linguistic distinction and it is not surprising that they are often found to be a source of difficulty for the dyslexic.

'Directional confusion' and the written language

The preceding discussion should have made it clear why we think that the problems of 'spatial and directional confusion' which have traditionally been thought to be root causes of dyslexic difficulties should not be regarded as defects of a special faculty called 'orientation' at all but merely as one facet of an underlying disorder of language. Vellutino (1979) has concluded in a similar vein that 'spatial and directional confusion is not a significant cause of reading disability' and goes on to question 'the very existence of this disorder as it has been discussed in the literature'. The underlying impairment can be expected to affect written language especially for two distinct but related reasons;

1. The problem which the dyslexic has over arbitrary/conventional links will be most severe where the link itself is at its most arbitrary, that is where the object referred to is itself both arbitrary and uncertain. The object

[picture of kettle]

which we chose for an earlier example is reassuringly solid and can be trusted to 'hold still' for purposes of naming, but there is much less certainty about *left and right*, which are arbitrary and abstract and which, moreover, 'fluctuate' in their meaning from moment to moment. One person's left is another person's right ('my' right, 'your' right) and the assignment of left and right switches as one turns one's back (see Miles and Ellis in Pavlidis and Miles, 1981, p. 223).

2. An alphabetic writing system depends on an exactly regulated stepwise progression from left to right, with skips from line to line.[5] It therefore demands a precise and developed perception of the left/right distinction to guarantee that we decode linguistic symbols in the order corresponding to the grapheme–phoneme relationship. In a less obvious way it is probable that an enhanced perception of left/right may also be the *result* of proficiency in writing and reading and therefore less well developed in dyslexic readers. The suggestion here is that as we become proficient in reading and writing, an interplay or exchange of skills takes place so that the skilful reader first defines and then increases and reinforces and finally stabilises his or her perception of left and right (and no doubt other skills as well) as

part of an overall learning process. Thus, an uncertainty over the linguistic categories of left and right may be both a cause and a consequence of a disorder of visible language function. Both aspects would need to be taken into account in devising a teaching programme.

Sequence

The basic insecurity discussed above could also be responsible for the general difficulties over spatial sequence and order which are so characteristic of the dyslexic child.

Memory

Our view of dyslexia avoids the need to construct a special defect of short-term memory which uniquely affects dyslexics. The difficulty that dyslexics certainly do have in remembering can be explained quite naturally and economically as being partly linguistic and partly psychological, with an accelerating interaction between the two. If one accepts that written words are for dyslexics especially random and unstable, it would be quite surprising if they found them easy to remember. Any residual problem of forgetting can be explained as the result of a growing sense of inadequacy in a fundamental human and social activity. 'Good memory' is largely a matter of confidence in one's own faculty and strategy.

Reading the Time

This problem combines several points of difficulty. First, there is the highly arbitrary and conventional relationship between the linear passage of time and the circular progression of hands round a clock – we have suggested that relationships of this kind are likely to cause problems for the dyslexic. Second, there is the problem of left/right orientation. Reading the time means knowing that as one faces 12 o'clock, time passes to the right, clockwise, not to the left. Finally, there is the 'reading' problem of decoding digits.

Colour Naming

To a much greater extent than is generally recognised, the perception of colour is a question of *language*. It is not the case that red, for instance, is universally identified as 'red', or blue as 'blue'; but, on the contrary, different cultures divide the spectrum of visible radiations into different segments for purposes of naming. A frequently cited example is the Welsh word *glas*, normally 'blue' but applied by Welsh speakers to some colour tones that English speakers would call 'green'. A glance at any paint manufacturer's colour cards will remind us how significant a role 'naming' plays in our perception of colour. It will be reasonable to assume that any difficulties which dyslexics have over colour naming will be a problem of language and not of visual perception, and one that will be heightened by general lack of confidence.

Other Problems: Multiplication tables, months of the year, difficulty over logical organisation of ideas, difficulty in repeating back long words, clumsiness.

These are, once again, *interacting* problems in which associated difficulties exert a heightening effect on one another. *Multiplication tables* are a problem because they demand in an unusual way the very skill that the dyslexic is weakest in – the ability to *name* rather than to *use* numbers. The nature of the disability means the dyslexic will find the first task harder than the second; it is a fact of experience that dyslexics are quite often good mathemeticians.

Months of the year again tax in a rather unusual way the skill of *naming*, and again the thing named is invisible. That the names have to be repeated in a special order no doubt heightens the difficulty.

Logical ordering of ideas. This problem generally comes to light when the older dyslexic is asked to construct essays. It could be explained in several language-related ways that are not inconsistent with one another: first, the ability to organise ideas into a logical progression is a developed skill that unfolds with the educational process; second, there is a mutual and progressive *interaction* between language and structure in that our ability to make use of language derives from an inbuilt mental structure (which may be weakened in the dyslexic) and, more importantly, in that our sense of structure is reciprocally sharpened through our developing use of language – written language in particular. Thus, the dyslexic, doubly unfortunate, is deprived both of the structure itself and of the useful consequences of having it. Difficulty in *repeating back long words* is evidently a language-related problem.

Clumsiness. It is not clear that this difficulty is characteristic of dyslexia. Where it does appear in a dyslexic child, it may be expected that it would be heightened by lack of confidence and a general insecurity about the linguistically controlled aspects of direction.

Notes

[1] Miles (1983).
[2] See p. 161 for some remarks about the pronunciation of consonant letters.

[3] 'A major shift in spelling occurs when children realise that sounds in the names of letters correspond to sounds they detect in the pronunciations of **words**' (L.C.Ehri in Snowling and Thomson, 1991, p. 68).

[4] Made visible by Miss Y during her California experience, pp. 17–18.

[5] This is not to say that the elements of the system are necessarily *processed* in this way.

Chapter 6
Linguistics and dyslexia

The ingredients of a linguistically based approach

Introduction

We begin this concluding section by recalling (see p. 26) that teachers and parents are constrained not only by the special needs of the dyslexic child, but also by the more general requirements of effective teaching. A linguistically based approach must therefore justify itself pedagogically as well as theoretically and it is able to do so very convincingly because it allows insights about *language* and insights about *teaching* to be brought together in a particularly natural and effective way.

Some Principles of Effective Teaching

1. Understand the underlying logic of the subject.
2. Set the student tasks that he or she is able to perform. This implies that the subject-matter will be structured into a finely graded progression, with each step building on the last.
3. Teaching/learning should be multi-dimensional.
4. Learning should be an active process.

These principles suggest the following comments.

1. *Underlying logic.* For us, dyslexia is a disorder of language which therefore provides the logical substrate.
2. *Progression.* Language, being itself a highly structured entity, is well adapted to a structured and graduated approach and such an approach can easily be developed within the context of existing *structured phonic programmes*. The application of this principle forms the main topic of Book Two.
3. *Multi-dimensional learning.* Essentially, this means that, as far as

52

possible, every facet of the student's personality and sensory apparatus should be engaged in the learning process. This has always been a recognised component of enlightened teaching practice. The term *multi-sensory approach* has been adopted for more recent formalisations directed particularly to the sensory inputs of sight, hearing, touch, smell and taste. In successful learning these *inputs* will be translated into *outputs*, the five activities of *thinking, doing, reading, writing, and speaking.* An effective lesson will allow space for all five activities and will switch rhythmically between them (Figure 16).

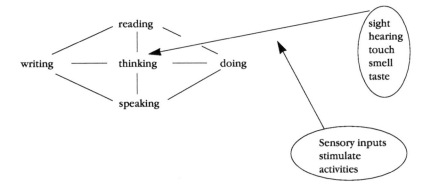

Figure 16. Structure of an effective lesson.

4. *Activity.* Activity assists the learning process in several ways. In particular, it operates as an effective way of 'fixing' the matter to be learned. Since dyslexics are at a disadvantage when linguistic material has to be 'fixed', every resource should be brought to bear in helping them with this task.

The Contributions of Linguistics

Linguistics makes its impact at two levels; first, at the level of *attitudes*; and, second, at the level of *procedures*.

Attitudes

An analogy

A space traveller has been marooned on Planet X, whose inhabitants spend the greater part of their time playing a subtle and extremely elaborate game. The rules of the game are intricate, but the people of the planet receive most of the necessary knowledge at birth as part of their genetic endowment. The remainder is supplied to them in infancy and early childhood.

Since the inhabitants regard their game as the main business of life, it is obviously necessary for the space traveller to learn it as quickly as possible, but there is a difficulty, or rather there are two difficulties.

First, the extreme complexity of the rules means that learning them will be a long and arduous business; however, the people of Planet X are willing to co-operate in any way they can.

The second difficulty is more serious. Since their knowledge of the rules is largely instinctive (genetically programmed), the inhabitants are only vaguely aware:

> that the rules exist,
>
> what they are like,
>
> what they are.

It follows that the inhabitants must in a sense 'learn' or 'discover' the rules themselves before they can pass them on to an alien. This branch of knowledge is still in its infancy on Planet X.

Although the analogy is not exact (the resources available to help the dyslexic 'alien' on this planet are far from being unlimited), its implications are broadly correct. Linguistic knowledge (still not very widespread) does enable us to enter into the dyslexic predicament to some extent, and perhaps this is its greatest single contribution. The linguistically informed teacher knows that reading is a complex process drawing on correspondingly sophisticated insights which may not be readily accessible to children whose genetic endowment is even slightly out of the ordinary. Such a teacher will be disinclined to tell the pupil not to make 'silly' or 'obvious' mistakes and may be better able to penetrate (in a sympathetic way) the barriers the dyslexic puts up to conceal his or her deficiencies and also to suggest ways of overcoming them.

Procedures

Linguistics *externalises* the interior rules of language, including those that are weakest in the dyslexic, and so makes it possible to teach them in a principled and systematic way. This matter is dealt with at length in Book Three; meanwhile, some general suggestions are given below.

The Written Language

As far as the teaching of literacy is concerned, the written language can be regarded as a device for turning the sounds of /*words*/ into groups of letters, the same letter group always being used to represent the same /*word*/. In the pedagogical tradition, the child has been required to demonstrate its mastery of the device by turning written symbols back into sounds, by reading them aloud in fact. However, the business of turning /word/ into <word> and back again gives rise to all kinds of difficulties which, as we know, bear particularly hard on the dyslexic. These difficulties may, in turn, suggest remedial opportunities:

a. First, there is the question of the nature and scope of the spoken /*word*/. Words, as we have seen, are arbitrary and conventional objects, in no way 'given' in the natural world. More surprisingly, they are not 'given' in *spoken language* either, which contains no pauses or other signals to demarcate the beginnings and ends of /words/. We do not, for instance, make any distinction *in speech* between 'inner tension' and 'inattention' or between 'debtor nation' and 'detonation'.[1] Instead, spoken language concerns itself with the divisions between longer units such as 'tunes', 'breath groups' and 'sentences'.

Part of *not* being dyslexic is that we have, nevertheless, some idea of what a /word/ is and a very clear perception of where /words/ begin and end in speech. How we arrive at these perceptions is mysterious and it would be quite wrong to assume that they are equally present to the dyslexic, whose training should therefore include an exploration of the *nature and boundaries of spoken words*: perhaps by being asked to report the number of words and syllables in a phrase *spoken* by the teacher. Purposeful conversation (as well as the informal kind) has an important part to play in the teaching of the dyslexic child.

b. Second, one must take cognisance of the fact that written language demands an analysis of each /*word*/ into a succession of *separate* sounds which are complexly ordered in speech, but which progress from left to right in (our) writing system. This analysis, like the separating-out of words themselves, is artificial, is not directly projected in ordinary speech, and may be entirely non-obvious to the dyslexic. Accordingly, each lesson should dedicate a few moments to an exercise in which the student slices written <words> into the components that represent each corresponding sound unit in the spoken word. Thus <c> <a> <t> contains three letters which each could be said to represent one sound in the spoken word /kaet/, where each division forms a spelling unit. This exercise can be quite revealing to teachers and pupils, especially if time is given to discussion of the various difficulties that will arise. The words chosen

c	a	t
k	æ	t

Similarly with

ea	ch	l	e	ss	o	n	s	ou	n	d	s	sh	oul	d
i	tʃ	l	ɛ	s	ə	n	s	aʊ	n	d	z	ʃ	ʊ	d
					n					z				

should be adapted to the pupil's stage of knowledge. It is not necessary always to arrive at a correct academic solution to the problem; the point of the exercise lies in the attempt.

Reversals or palindromes make a good word exercise for sharpening the student's perception of word segmentation. The teacher says a word

a l o u d   and the pupil repeats it   a l o u d

backwards to make a different word. More advanced students can discuss the way this process works in the *written* language – spelling changes will sometimes be needed. Here are some palindromes.

tab	kit	luke
tub	muck	tool
tea	loop	gnat
ooze	puck	ten
mad	cope	bat
card	but	ark
tin	seep	net
fine	ken	

It must be emphasised that this is an exercise on sounds and it is the sounds and *not* the letters that are reversed. The reversal of *gnat* is *tan* not *tang*. The reversal of *muck* is *come*. The reversal of *seep* is ....?

c. Linguistics tells us that English speech relies on about 44 distinctively different sound units, but provides only 26 symbols for transcribing them into the written language, a piece of economising which necessitates the various combinations and groupings so familiar to the student of literacy.

This complex system is described in detail in Book Three; the point to be made here is that only linguistics provides an effective means of engaging with the relation between written and spoken language, describing its complexities (for the teacher) and mediating them (for the taught).

d. Linguistics has a healthy 'distancing' effect in relation to language, which prevents one from taking too much for granted and allows one to help the dyslexic in two somewhat related ways.

First, the dyslexic is likely to be partly unaware of the extent to which his 'alien' outlook differentiates him/her from other people who are not dyslexic. A linguistic approach allows for these differences and makes it possible to explore them and bring them to the surface of consciousness in a sensitive way.

Second, there are those 'cognitive discrepancies' of which the dyslexic is very well aware but has become adept at concealing. Linguistic insights combined with tact and sensitivity will make it possible for these deficiencies to be exposed and remediated. Among the concepts that are 'self-evident' to ordinary people but not to dyslexics are the following, which should be discussed and enacted as part of each lesson.

upside-down <ʍoιq>

right way up <word>,
right way round
wrong way round
back to front (say your name backwards – spell your name backwards)
word in wrong order <drwo>
word back to front <drow>

letters back to front <woιb>
        forwards
        backwards
        left (hand) side
        right (hand) side

left hand
right hand
your left
my left

e. *Contextual clues.* Even in the earlier stages of reading development, the child begins to make use of the linguistic clues that words supply for themselves and for other words. Examples of clues *within* a word would be *location of stress*; the child has to learn that <u> carries a different message in *supper*, where it is stressed, and in *supply*, where it is not. Similarly, with <a> in *apple* and *apply*, or the two <y>s in *shyly*.

Examples of linguistic clues *among* words would be the operation of familiar *word fragments* like

-ance (in *performance*)
-ity (in *simplicity*)
con- (in *control*)

which are extremely plentiful in English, and which serve to set up a network of grammatical nuance, which then assists in the prediction of meaning and pronunciation. 'Little words' like *the, her, a* and *she* serve the same function so that

in her dr

suggests a context in which the occurrence of dream is expectable but not the occurrence of *dreamt* and the pronunciation of <ea> is thereby predicted.

She dr

suggests a different context and a different pronunciation. The whole question of contextual clues is discussed in detail in Book Three.

f. *Activity and interactivity.*

'Reading as much as speech is essentially a language code utilised for communication between people' (Michael Rutter in Benton and Pearl, 1978, p. 7).

Because linguistics perceives language *primarily* as interaction and communication, the linguistically oriented parent/teacher can combine an insight from teaching (the value of activity) with an insight from linguistics (the interactive nature of written language) to justify and stimulate the development of all sorts of language-related games and activities in which several pupils can participate.

Some of these possibilities are explored in Book Two.

Conclusion

Linguistics teaches us first, that we ask the wrong questions about the dyslexic child and approach him/her from the wrong direction.

We ask why do dyslexics make a particular kind of spelling mistake? write <loin> for <lion>?

Я for **R** ?

When we should be asking, How do we, the normal majority, know that <lion> not <loin>

R and not **Я**

is the appropriate response in a given situation?

What mechanism enables us to form and retain a semi-automatic link between a large carnivorous animal and a particular (non-pictorial) arrangement of lines on a page? How is a failure of that link to be compensated for?

Linguistics teaches us, second, that progress in the remediation of dyslexia will come about not through the discovery of ideal methods or ideal treatments, but through a growth in the knowledge and understanding of parents and teachers which allows them to enter more fully into the dyslexic condition and to derive their teaching from an inner model that goes some way towards matching the complexities of written language and the reading process.[2]

Notes

[1] These examples will not work for dialects in which the <r>s get pronounced, but the same point can be made in those dialects too. Fish and tea – Fission T; massive incongruities – mass of incongruities.

[2] Such a model is supplied in Book Three.

Book Two
Immediate
Problems and
Strategies

Where to start and what to do

Background and introduction

The first draft of this book was written in 1985. At that time, the authors' reactions to the 1981 Education Act were seen as somewhat pessimistic. Also, some educationalists felt that our proposals for self-help initiatives were both unnecessary and inappropriate.

A decade later, it would be difficult to deny the realities of the 'Special Educational Needs' situation. Resources are limited, awareness courses for parents are on the increase, dyslexia tests are available for home consumption and increasingly large numbers of teachers and parents are taking matters and responsibilities into their own hands.

Furthermore, ten years on, evidence from parents and classroom teachers indicates that ever-growing numbers of language-disabled pupils have made progress when structured language programmes and multi-sensory teaching methods have been implemented. That so many pupils have made progress will not surprise informed educationalists; structured language programmes are underwritten by linguistic research and evidence suggests that even inexperienced parents/teachers quickly learn to appreciate and teach the basic principles. This being so, there seems no good reason why pupils should not be taught the sounds, structures and systems of the mother tongue as soon as language problems become evident; the alternative is increasing confusion and frustration pending the often long-awaited visit from 'a specialist'.

We return, then, to the observed needs of parents and teachers, and clearly their views on self-help shaped the original package. To acknowledge this is to admit that the original decision *not* to write and include a programme covering the teaching of reading, writing and spelling was, to some extent, taken for us. Many interested teachers and parents sought expertise rather than yet another programme necessary and we were aware that the best programmes were beyond significant improvement. We also believe that we were right to focus on *Alpha to Omega.*

New readers may be interested to know that the text includes a linguistics/phonetics component and also deals with those aspects of dyslexia most frequently mentioned by other informed parties. Parents, teachers, members of local dyslexia associations, psychologists and children were all consulted. The dyslexic's social, emotional and intellectual problems are described and discussed in some detail, as are essential linguistic priorities. A practical approach to self-help has been a constant consideration, the writers attempting throughout to maintain a realistic and dyslexia-centred position.

Inevitably, problems of selection and separation remain. The reader will perhaps appreciate that it has proved difficult to describe separately each of the interacting manifestations of the dyslexia syndrome; nor has it been possible to distinguish precisely between the different aspects of remediation. Some chapters will be found to overlap, particular themes emerging in other parts of the text.

It is suggested that parents and teachers read this entire book, even though some chapters are ostensibly more relevant to one party or the other. A mutually supportive home/school environment is accepted as being beneficial; if teachers and parents appreciate one another's problems, objectives and perspectives, the dyslexic pupil concerned will almost certainly gain. It may also perhaps be worth mentioning that language students in teacher training establishments and colleges of education might find Chapters 4 and 5 helpful to their studies.

Chapter 1 answers some of the questions commonly asked by parents and teachers. The question/answer format is used to present basic information for the benefit of anyone who has had little previous experience of dyslexia. Chapter 2 is a case study which might help parents and teachers to identify and understand pupils suffering from the inherent disadvantages of dyslexia. The following chapter suggests ways in which teachers and parents might help dyslexics to practise and improve their skills in orientation, sequencing and memory. Chapter 4 discusses the concept of structure in relation to structured phonic programmes. (Most experts in dyslexia agree that an appreciation of structure is central to the success of such programmes and the exercises which follow the discussion are designed to enlighten those who are new to this concept.)

The penultimate chapter (5) examines testing, lesson planning and record keeping. Structured phonic tests are presented in detail, as are specific examples of lesson plans. Chapter 6 sets out some card and board games, useful ideas and so on, which have proved popular with dyslexic pupils. The aims of the games and details of construction are presented. Those principles discussed in earlier chapters inform the games which are provenly both effective and popular with dyslexic pupils.

Finally here, readers familiar with the first edition may care to note that chapters (1) and (6) have been substantially revised.

Chapter 1
Dyslexia: questions and answers

Introduction

This chapter arises from the authors' many discussions with teachers and parents. The authors attempt to deal with the most common enquiries and concerns, among them the particulars and practicalities of remediation.

Q1   What is dyslexia?

A   Dyslexia is generally accepted to be a partly unexplained delay or disorder of the language function. Some psychologists and educationists prefer the term 'Specific Learning Difficulty'. The subject is discussed further in Book One.

Q2   I have only read magazine articles about dyslexia but the children described sounded so much like my son that I am wondering whether he might be dyslexic. What should I do?

A   You need to talk to your child's class teacher and the head-teacher. Be prepared for a cautious, if not negative, response; attitudes and awareness vary and diagnosis can be difficult.

At this stage contact with your local dyslexia association (often listed as a Helpline in the local press or on file at the local library) and/or the British Dyslexia Association is useful; unless you are very fortunate you will almost certainly need independent advice and support at this time.

Q3   What causes dyslexia?

A   Opinions vary. Recent American studies suggest that dyslexia is associated with events in the womb at the time the brain is being formed. It has been posited that the cells relating to language development fail to end up in the right place. Investigations continue.

Q4   Assuming that my child is dyslexic, I need to know my rights. What are they?

A   A historical perspective is useful here. The 1981 Education Act fundamentally changed the law as far as dyslexic children were concerned; their disability was identified as one of many covered by the newly introduced concept of 'Special Educational Needs' (20% of children might be expected to fall into this category at some time during their school lives). However, many local education authorities had great difficulty with funding, and changes in provision and practice are–and have been – less substantial than was anticipated in some quarters.

However, a new Code of Practice attempts to modify the rather unwieldy procedural responses and circular arguments for which the 1981 Act was criticized.

In theory, the new procedure is more 'parent-friendly', simpler and speedier. It is structured by stages, the first two being school-based.

Q5   What does this mean, in real terms?

A   Briefly, that the school makes every attempt to identify and deal with any disparity between perceived potential and slow acquisition of literacy and numeracy skills.

The British Dyslexia Association (in *The 1993 Education Act and the Code of practice*, 1994) believes that 'many dyslexic children can have their needs met in school, without the need for a formal statement, provided that their school:
>   has identified their difficulties at an early age
>   fully understands all the problems involved
>   provides relevant and suitably skilled support
>   continually evaluates the effectiveness of the provision made.'

This is fine in theory, but there are difficulties. Again, resources are limited, and demand outstrips supply in many hard-pressed LEAs. Specialist training is expensive in terms of both time and money and, at present, many classroom teachers feel ill-equipped to offer 'suitably skilled support'.

Discussion of the general and particular consequences of limited investment in special education is inappropriate here.

None the less, reports from parents are interesting. For instance, the two-stage, school-based procedure is sometimes perceived as an exercise in procrastination and remediation is variously described as 'ineffective', 'just more of the same', 'patchy' and so forth. Given this state of affairs, a growing demand for external specialist intervention (stage 3) and/or statutory assessment is hardly surprising. The notion that effective remediation will quickly and automatically follow this external and formal recognition is common. However, from a parent's point of view, the formal procedure is not straightforward and again, contact with a local dyslexia association and/or the BDA is recommended.

In conclusion, experience suggests that a good deal of time can be wasted at all or any of the various stages. Self-taught skills or home-based remediation might offer a more immediate solution to the problem (see Q/As 16 to 27).

Q6　If the psychologist is called in, what will she or he do?

A　The psychologist tries to examine all the factors which affect the child's learning. This generally means the psychologist will administer a number of tests, one of them being a standard intelligence test.

Q7　How do dyslexic pupils perform on intelligence tests?

A　As far as can be ascertained, there is no correlation at all between dyslexia and intelligence; the syndrome has been identified in many different learning profiles. Having said that, dyslexic pupils often perform well on intelligence tests. Indeed, it is the disparity between assessed high intelligence and low reading age which sometimes convinces educationists of the reality of the disability.

The dyslexic child often shows a 'spiky' profile on general intelligence tests. For example, on the commonly used Wechsler Intelligence Scale for Children[1], poor performances in mental arithmetic, visual/motor coding, general knowledge and short-term auditory memory tasks contrast with high scores in other areas.

Q8　What is IQ and how is it possible to measure it?

A　IQ means Intelligence Quotient. In Western culture, certain abilities and skills are taken as manifestations of intelligence and psychologists have designed tests to measure these skills. Any new psychological test is itself tested stringently and the results of well-established tests are, for the most part, statistically reliable.

As regards IQ, then, this means that if a pupil appears to have 'average' abilities when sequencing/recalling items, defining words/concepts, co-ordinating visual and motor skills and so forth, his IQ would probably be around 100: that is 'average' for the general population.

Having said that, although high IQ carries conviction in some circumstances (see Q/A 7), it is the underlying pattern of abilities and difficulties that should inform remediation.

Q9   Is there a cure for dyslexia?
A   Not in the conventional or medical sense, but there is evidence that early recognition and intervention can help solve many of the dyslexic's practical, emotional and intellectual problems.

Children disabled by dyslexia can make very rapid progress if given specialist teaching; progress with reading, for example, sometimes being quite dramatically obvious. None the less, it must also be said that research also indicates that dyslexic pupils are unlikely to read and spell as well as other children of the same age and ability: 'Despite specialised teaching they could not catch up completely.'[2]

Q10   Can dyslexia be predicted?
A   Yes, to some extent, although many psychologists argue (as part of a wider debate)[3] that research and resources should be directed towards prevention rather than prediction.

Be that as it may, the informed observer will notice the signs and symptoms of dyslexia long before the emergence of the literacy problems usually associated with the syndrome.

Some of the early indications[4]

1   Difficulty with fastening his coat, shoelaces and tie.
2   Shoes often on the wrong feet, seemingly unaware that they are uncomfortable.
3   Appears to be clumsy or 'accident-prone'.
4   Difficulty hopping, skipping, or clapping a simple rhythm.
5   Difficulty throwing, catching or kicking a ball.
6   Difficulty understanding prepositions connected with direction, e.g. in/out, up/down, under/over, forwards/backwards.

7   Difficulty carrying out more than one instruction at a time.
8   Possible history of slow speech development.
9   Excessive spoonerisms, e.g. 'par car' for 'car park', 'beg and acorn' for 'egg and bacon'.
10 Difficulty in pronouncing multi-syllable words, e.g. 'hopsital' for 'hospital'.
11 Difficulty in finding the name for an object.
12 Confusion between left and right.
13 Undetermined hand preference.
14 Poor handwriting with many reversals and badly formed letters.
'5 Inability to copy accurately, particularly from the blackboard.
16 Difficulty remembering what day it is, when his birthday is, his address or his telephone number.
17 Difficulty learning to tell the time.
18 Unsure about 'yesterday' and 'tomorrow'.
19 Difficulty remembering anything in sequential order, e.g. days of the week, months of the year and multiplication tables.
20 Poor reading progress on both look-and-say and phonic methods.
21 Excessive tiredness due to of the amount of concentration and effort required, often for very little result.

Many of these points are still evident during the junior school years together with more specific reading and writing errors. One of the difficulties of diagnosis is that these signs vary and occur in many different combinations. Mothers comparing notes about their dyslexic children's early history find many similarities but also some marked differences. Perhaps the most useful advice relates to disparity: parents and teachers should note discrepancies – any difficulty or failure that does not match the more usual level of performance.

Interestingly, many teachers/parents of older dyslexics recall an awareness of this disparity in performance but report problems when trying to explain their observations to others.

To summarise, then, it seems that the dyslexic often has problems with tasks which involve all or any of the following:

a. Orientation–distinguishing between left/right, top/bottom, front/back, up/down, in/out and so on.

b. Visual/temporal/auditory sequencing – (putting items/events in a particular order).

c. Short-term recall of instructions/items, particularly if the information is only transmitted once and/or the required actions do not

match the order of instruction. (Instructions such as 'Turn to pa
14, make notes on the second paragraph and don't forget to put t
date at the top of the page', can be particularly confusing for
dyslexic student.)

Problems in these areas may be exacerbated by reading failu
and loss of confidence. It is also worth mentioning that the incidenc
of dyslexia appears to be four times as likely in boys as in girls an
that a family history of these sorts of difficulties may be a pointer.

Finally, readers might be interested to know of the Inner Sens
Dyslexia Test[5] which has been designed for home use and is said to
have been developed from assessment material currently used by
specialist teachers.

Q11   What practical tasks might the young dyslexic find particularly
         difficult and why?
A   Any task which involves the skills mentioned above. The
         dyslexic may forget to bring all the items he is told to bring
         from the shop. He might mix up the order of garments when
         dressing, confusing 'under' and 'over' garments, putting
         buttons in the wrong buttonholes and so on. Dressing involves
         a numbers of small tasks which have to be performed in a
         certain order. The skills required may, at first sight, seem very
         basic but major concepts are involved here. Many of us
         employ a silent naming strategy when dealing with such tasks.
         Tying shoelaces, for example, can involve a great deal of
         naming. ('Is it left to right or vice versa? Top to bottom or
         bottom to top? Which lace do I loop over first to start the
         bow?') A dyslexic may well find it difficult to learn, name and
         accurately recall all the patterns of activities which make life
         run more smoothly for most of us. (It is hardly surprising that
         he has difficulty remembering the order and orientation of
         'meaningless' shapes which we call letters.)
         (*Note*: It might be useful at this point to read the case study in
         Chapter 2.)
Q12   Why can the dyslexic recall what happened on his holidays last
         year but forget the date which I have just told him?
A   There seems to be a difference in the processing here. Long-
         term memory is commonly agreed to be episodic, more to do
         with meaning than with the processing of language, and
         dyslexics are notoriously weak when it comes to language.
Q13   Why and how does the dyslexic's language development differ
         from that of his peers?

A   The typical dyslexic appears to be disabled by a 'phonological deficit' and, inevitably, this affects acquisition language in one way or another.

It seems that most children are born with an innate potential to exploit the language they hear. For example, they quickly learn to discriminate between word, syllables and individual sounds. This is no small achievement given that most utterances are merely long streams of sound. There are, in fact, some 44 sounds in the English language and amazingly, most young children acquire them with little difficulty. A child must learn – and be able to use and manipulate – all these sounds if s/he is to achieve full linguistic competence.

Dyslexics seem to have more difficulty with discrimination than most. Also, often disadvantaged by loss of confidence in his/her ordering and memory skills, the dyslexic may 'lose' sounds before they are stored for future use. An analogy may be useful: imagine a room with open doors at either end, a gale blowing through and lots of packs of cards scattered all over. The child's task is to sort the cards into ordered packs of 44 while the wind is constantly moving the cards about. Small wonder that the dyslexic may be slow to acquire his/her native tongue. 'Normal' peer will have fewer problems.

Q14 But why does the dyslexic have difficulty in learning to read, write and spell?

A   The reasons are very similar to those given above. Additionally, there seems to be a problem with *visual* discrimination, access to and accurate recall of stored word 'pictures'. The printed word is a representation of those sounds which the dyslexic may have had difficulty in learning. Many reading schemes present combinations of visual symbols (words) quite indiscriminately and most pupils can cope with this. They remember the 'look' of the word, the order of the letters and can accurately and easily relate this 'picture' to the 'name' of the word. Typically, the pupil is shown a flash card of the whole word and he responds to it immediately. Also, most pupils discriminate and store the correspondences between individual sounds and letters with little difficulty. Dyslexics, disadvantaged by the inherent weaknesses already described, often have difficulty in dealing with this new dimension of language. Learning to read and write demands and extends skills in discrimination, memory, access and ordering at both auditory and visual levels. Often dyslexics cannot process the complex combinations of symbols presented by reading schemes. They find it difficult to produce accurate 'pictures' of whole words and to work out the correspondence between individual sounds and letters.[6]

To summarise, some dyslexics seem to get stuck at the logographic stage (a word is merely a logo or picture) and the development of others appears to be arrested at the alphabetic stage. (The child begins to understand the relationship between the letters of the alphabet and sounds as embodied in the printed word but his performance is unreliable.)

Given that transition to the final orthographic stage derives from a combination of logographic and alphabetic strategies, it is difficult for a dyslexic to achieve full linguistic competence through his own efforts. The vast majority of dyslexics need help from a specialist.

Q15 Are there different degrees of dyslexia?

A   Yes. Some dyslexics learn to talk easily but have difficulty with reading. Others learn to read but find spelling a problem. Different degrees and manifestations of dyslexia can be apparent in many situations. For example: the dyslexic may have battled his/her way through learning to read and write but s/he still has great difficulty in learning times tables, remembering lists of items, writing précis or taking lecture notes.

Q16 What sort of language programme is likely to be most suitable for the dyslexic who is failing at reading and spelling?

A   Research suggests that a structured phonic programme suits many dyslexics best. A good phonic programme is comprehensive, cumulative and structured. It is also sequential in the sense that the pupil is never asked to write anything he has not previously been taught. Such programmes (unlike 'Look and Say' reading schemes, for example) do not rely on a well-developed visual memory. Generally authors of structured phonic programmes do not make assumptions about powers of discrimination, ordering and memory. The pupil is taught how the sounds of the language relate to the 26 letters of the Roman alphabet. This is not as straightforward as it seems; the language uses a variety of strategies to relate the 26 letters of the alphabet to the 44 sounds. (For example, the language does not use a single letter to represent the medial sound in CR*E*AM.) Structured phonic programmes are quite explicit in that they demonstrate how each of the 44 sounds relates to its written representation. The pupil is not expected to remember long strings of letter shapes and their order; the best structured phonic programmes teach the pupil to identify the shapes of letters and to relate them to their sounds. S/he is then shown how to build the parts which make up a whole word. A structured way of teaching parts rather than whole relies on a step-by-step approach; this reduces the strain on memory, ordering and discrimination. For instance, thinking of the word *STEAL,* the pupil would be taught the initial blended sound (represented by *ST),* the medial long vowel sound (represented by *EA)* and the final sound (represented by *L).* He would then be asked to read and write only words which contained sound(s)/letter(s) patterns with which he was familiar (*least, seal, eat, east, eats).* Each of the three 'bits' would be reinforced by dictation, reading and exercises. Thus the pupil learns to respond quickly to these small patterns which do not over-tax his memory; the patterns are stored for future retrieval.

Q17 Could one of these structured phonic programmes be used successfully in the home situation?

A Yes, provided the parent/child relationship is good and the parent has acquired an understanding of the principles involved. Some parents may feel apprehensive about teaching their own children, but once the dyslexic is convinced that home teaching will help any tensions usually diminish. There are several structured phonic programmes available. (A particularly straightforward one is *Alpha to Omega,* by Hornsby and Shear (1974): see Background and Introduction, pp. 64–4.)

As the step-by-step approach of such programmes generally brings early success, dyslexics usually become highly motivated and committed to their home lessons. It must be emphasised, however, that the authors of some programmes assume linguistic expertise and many parents and teachers do not have access to the appropriate resources – hence the present text.

Q18 Would there by any risk of home teaching causing confusion in relation to school?

A In the authors' view, very little.

Structured phonic programmes are commonly based on carefully researched facts about language. Almost everything the child is taught will be relevant, at some point, to the reading and writing he does at school. Of course, the school reading scheme may not be as structured as the home programme. Nevertheless, the 'bits' of structure taught at home will help a pupil in the classroom situation. For example: imagine the pupil has been taught the letters/sound correspondence IGH as in NIGHT at home. He will probably be able to read the large number of common words containing this letter sequence as it occurs in the school's reading book.

Q19 What teaching method is most suitable for dyslexics?

A   The method described as multisensory. This means that the senses of touch, vision, and hearing are all simultaneously involved in the learning process, any weak neurological linkages being connected to stronger ones. One of the reasons for the proven success of this method may be that the memory is over-impressed with information which is stored. The diagrams which follow illustrate the principles underpinning the multisensory method. Notice that diagram A shows the position when all the sensory channels are operating efficiently. Diagrams B1, B2, B3 and B4 set out and explain the significantly different situations which arise when any one of the four sensory channels fails to connect with the others.

A

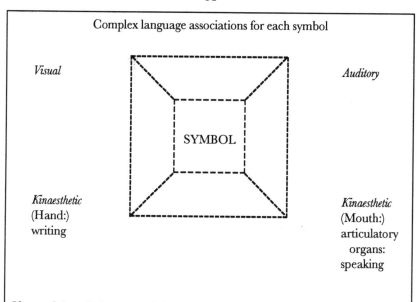

Complex language associations for each symbol

Visual

Auditory

SYMBOL

Kinaesthetic
(Hand:)
writing

Kinaesthetic
(Mouth:)
articulatory
organs:
speaking

If any of these linkages are defective there will be corresponding defects in the language function.

Adapted from: *Assessment and Teaching of Dyslexic Children.* London: ICAA (1973) A.G. Wolff.

B1

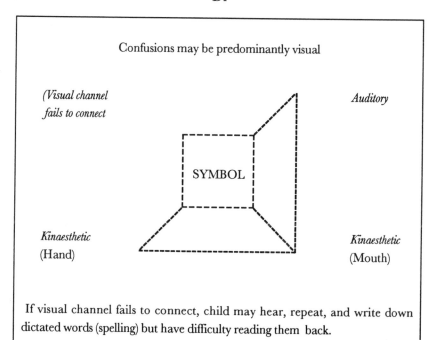

Confusions may be predominantly visual

*(Visual channel
fails to connect*

Auditory

SYMBOL

Kinaesthetic
(Hand)

Kinaesthetic
(Mouth)

If visual channel fails to connect, child may hear, repeat, and write down dictated words (spelling) but have difficulty reading them back.

Adapted from: *Assessment and Teaching of Dyslexic Children.* London: ICAA (1973) A.G. Wolff.

B2

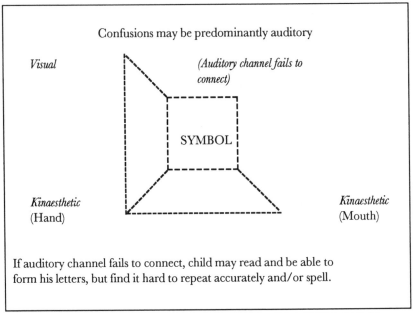

Confusions may be predominantly auditory

Visual

(Auditory channel fails to connect)

SYMBOL

Kinaesthetic
(Hand)

Kinaesthetic
(Mouth)

If auditory channel fails to connect, child may read and be able to form his letters, but find it hard to repeat accurately and/or spell.

Adapted from: *Assessment and Teaching of Dyslexic Children.* London: ICAA (1973) A.G. Wolff.

B3

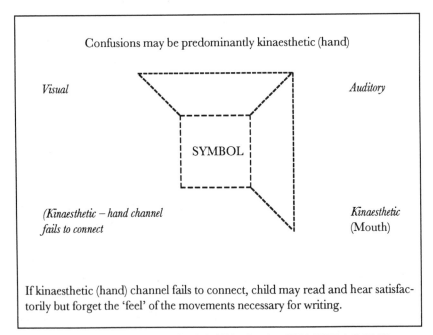

Confusions may be predominantly kinaesthetic (hand)

Visual

Auditory

SYMBOL

*(Kinaesthetic – hand channel
fails to connect*

Kinaesthetic
(Mouth)

If kinaesthetic (hand) channel fails to connect, child may read and hear satisfactorily but forget the 'feel' of the movements necessary for writing.

Adapted from: *Assessment and Teaching of Dyslexic Children.* London: ICAA (1973) A.G. Wolff.

B4

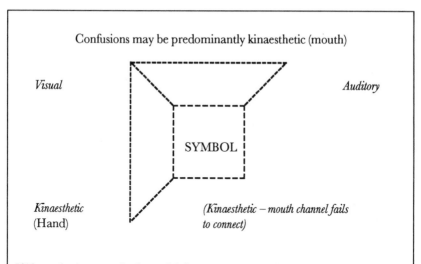

Confusions may be predominantly kinaesthetic (mouth)

Visual

Auditory

SYMBOL

Kinaesthetic
(Hand)

(Kinaesthetic – mouth channel fails
to connect)

If kinaesthetic – mouth channel fails to connect, child may hear, write and spell satisfactorily but have difficulty organising the articulatory organs (speech).

Adapted from: *Assessment and Teaching of Dyslexic Children*. London: ICAA (1973) A.G. Wolff.

Q20 Will the pupil find it difficult to adapt to this teaching method?
A No. It is perfectly straightforward and many pupils very quickly become used to it.

Hornsby and Shear's 'multisensory drill' is particularly explicit and the procedure detailed below is based on their original recommendations.

1 Teacher presents letter written on flash card with key picture drawn on reverse side; pupil says the letter's name.
2 Teacher says the key word and then the sound of the letter.
3 Pupil repeats key word and sound.
4 Teacher says the sound and then the name.
5 Pupil repeats the sound and gives name, writing it as he says it. (He is translating the sounds heard into written letters.)
6 Pupil reads what he has written, giving sound. (He is translating the letters written into sounds, linking the independent but related skills of reading and spelling.)
7 Pupil writes letter with eyes closed to get the feel of the letter.

It is suggested that at stages 5 and 6 the pupil is also encouraged to try to locate the precise point of articulation; he should try to identify which part of the mouth – palate, tongue, lips – shapes the sound. You might feel unsure about locating this point yourself – although keen observation and a mirror help. Hornsby and Shear also recommend the use of the *Edith Norrie Letter Case*, which identifies the common articulatory features of certain sounds.

Finally, some advice based on experience: given that this drill quickly becomes routine, there may be a temptation to depart from/vary the set procedure. The general principles of multisensory activity have already been mentioned and it is important that their application is maintained.

Q21 I think I see the reason for multisensory teaching methods, but why is there such an emphasis on letter tiles, wooden letters, letters on bits of card and so forth?

A   First, this is part of the *multisensory* method. Also, there is a notion that the physical manipulation of letters of the alphabet (on card, tile or whatever) moves progress from the logographic to the alphabetic phase (see Q/A 14): the child starts to appreciate the role and significance of individual letters and begins to learn sound/letter correspondences.

Q22 Do dyslexics also have problems with maths and why?

A   Many (but not all) dyslexics have problems with maths. This is not so surprising given that the subject requires (among other things) good sequencing and recall skills. Times tables, procedures and so on are central features of mathematics and often a problem for dyslexics.

Having said that, specialist books[7] and videos[8] now offer a way forward.

Q23 Assuming I have access to, or have purchased, a structured phonic programme such as *Alpha to Omega*, where do I begin?

A   It is recommended that you start by doing the diagnostic tests presented in Chapter 5 of this section. You will then be in a position to plan your first lesson in accordance with the principles set out there.

Q24 What about reading books? Is there such a thing as a structured reading scheme?

A   Structure as defined in this context is not usually a feature of conventional reading schemes. If the pupil is mildly dyslexic this may not be a problem; he might be in a position to choose from a number of recommended series.[9]

On the other hand, if the pupil is really struggling, it may be better in the short term to forget about reading books.

If neither of these solutions appeals, there are a couple of schemes[10] in which the language is as structured, cumulative and progressive as is possible in the context of the various stories.

Q25   In what other practical ways can the pupil be helped?

A   You might try the Activities and Strategies explained in Chapter 3 and the games presented in Chapter 6.

Q26   Would it help the pupil if he were told that he was dyslexic?

A   Yes, it probably would. Adult dyslexics tell us that being identified was not a disadvantage; that on the contrary it generally led to positive and specific help. Furthermore, these same adults point out that counselling and discussion about the practical consequences of dyslexia (see Q/As 10 and 11) helped them to come to terms with their inherent disadvantages.

Q27   What about dyslexics and computers?

A   The Computer Committee of the British Dyslexia Association will supply literature and the Dyslexia Computer Resource Centre[11] maintains a database.

If *Alpha to Omega* is used and an **IBM**-compatible PC is available, 'WordShark' from WhiteSpace is excellent.

Notes

[1] WISC Test: NFER/Nelson.

[2] Study conducted for the Dyslexia Institute: 1993/94 (John Rack) Dyslexics still slower despite extra lessons, *The Guardian*, 3 November 1994.

[3] Bryant, P. (1990) Children's Written Language Difficulties, edited by Snowling, M.J. Windsor: NFER/Nelson.

[4] Augur, Jean. *Children's Written Language Difficulties*, NFER/Nelson.

[5] Inner Sense Development Centre, 39 Lickfold's Road, Rowledge, Farnham, Surry CU104AE

[6] A model of the leading process can be found in *Children's Written Language Difficultes*. NFER/NELSON: (Edit) Snowling: The assessment of Reading and spelling skills.

[7] Henderson, A, *Maths and Dyslexia* (St. David's College, Llandudno), is recommended as a starting-point.

[8] Sharma, M.C., *Learning Difficulties and Maths* (videos I and II, Computer Resource Centre, University of Hull.

[9] See list in *Alpha to Omega*.

[10] *For younger children*, Birkett, R., *Sounds Easy Series*, Egon (Baldock, Herts); *For early teens/language disabled adults:* Evans and Henton, *Pam and Tom Series*, Focus Trading Ltd (Barnsley College, Barnsley, S. Yorks).

[11] Department of Psychology, University of Hull, Hull HU67 RX. Telephone: 01482–465589.

Chapter 2
Case study: John B

Introduction

John B is the pseudonym of a real child, a child who is in many (but not all) respects typically dyslexic. Parents whose children are affected by the dyslexia syndrome will find much that is familiar and, hopefully, reassuring here, but this is not the only objective of this discussion. The study is intended for all those adults who have ever been puzzled by the wide variety of intellectual, emotional and practical manifestations of dyslexia. Whether these manifestations stem from one or a variety of causes remains unclear but experience suggests that John B's pattern of difficulties is not unusual. If this account of his problems and history improves understanding and persuades those involved with dyslexics to set more realistic goals – for themselves and their pupils – it will satisfy its main purpose.

The account is based on material gathered over a period of three years. Throughout that time John B was taught once a week by the writer on a one-to-one basis. A post-lesson discussion with John and/or various members of his family was a frequent feature of these weekly meetings. Such discussion offered a unique opportunity to learn about dyslexia *in situ*.

As a final word, it is perhaps worth mentioning that John and his family endorse and approve of this study.

Background

John's parents are both quiet unassuming people who seem content with their family-centred life. John's mother was in charge of the footwear department of a large store by the time she married, having progressed from the junior assistant position she took up at 15. She resigned her senior position three months before John was born and has not worked since. John's father was manager of a tailoring department at the time of John's parents' first meeting. Mr B has changed jobs twice since then and is a driver/inspector for a local bus company.

Mrs B thinks she did 'quite well at school' until a serious health problem began to interfere with her education. She attended school only very intermittently between the ages of 11 and 15, long periods of hospitalisation making it impossible for her to keep up with her classmates.

John's father has always had problems with spelling and – to a lesser extent – reading. He feels that difficulties in this area affected his school progress considerably.

John was born on 26 February 1970 and his mother, who was 26 at the time, remembers her pregnancy as 'straightforward'. The birth itself, however, was quite difficult, John eventually being delivered by forceps. He was a full-term baby and his parents' only child until his brother was born three years later.

Mr and Mrs B looked forward to the births of both their children. Although they each have their own domestic-centred interests, they also take – and have always taken – a lively interest in their children's activities. Family holidays, for instance, usually include birdwatching trips, visits to history museums and so on. These excursions being followed up by visits to the local library, and reading of special magazines and periodicals.

Early history

John's early development appears to have been in advance of average expectation and, in some respects, he seems to have been very significantly forward for his age.

John's mother remembers he was 'about right' as regards teething and feeding himself, but he did walk rather early – at exactly 10 months. Also control over other body movements – running, climbing upstairs, clapping and so on – seems to have been evident unusually early.

Mrs B also recalls that John was a singularly healthy toddler. His first real illness was German measles, which he did not contract until he was nine, and his only illness since (apart from the occasional cold) has been chicken-pox.

John's parents remember being especially surprised at his language development. Apparently, he bypassed the 'one-word, short-phrase' stage completely, his first intelligible speech being in the form of complete and sometimes complex sentences. Mrs B has often wondered how much John's language development was affected by his close relationship with his resident grandmother, who spent long periods talking with the toddler.

John also seems to have been exceptionally good at space relationships and what psychologists call space-adaptive behaviour; from an early age he could locate his toys in cupboards and other rooms, distinguish between wooden shapes when building castles, cars, and so on, and was extremely good at jigsaws. John's mother believes that, at this stage, he definitely favoured his left hand and foot.

John's social adaptive behaviour seems to have been equally unusual. Apparently, he has always had (and continues to have) a calm and somewhat stoical temperament, rarely demanding and (up to the time of writing) bypassing the 'rebellious' and 'reckless' teenage stages predicted by psychologists.

Mrs B recalls that John would always play happily by himself, thinking about and organising a task before he attempted to do it. John's parents saw such behaviour as manifestations of early maturity and, until he started school, were quietly confident that John was a 'bright little boy'.

Later development and problems

John started school when he was five. His mother was not worried about his ability to cope generally but she *was* concerned about one or two things. For instance, at five, John was still unable to tie his shoelaces, despite on both his and his mother's best efforts. Also, surprisingly for a child who was so advanced in other ways, John seemed unable to grasp even the basic principles involved in telling the time.

However, John seemed to settle quite well at school and his mother had few worries until she realised that John was the only child she knew who was not bringing home a reading book. During this period Mrs B herself had been trying to interest John in reading, but without success. He appeared to quite enjoy being read to but could not identify words for himself, even though his mother pointed at and pointed out some words time and time again.

Mrs B, not wishing to appear over-anxious, did not approach school until John was turned six. John's teacher told Mrs B that there could be cause for anxiety, but that equally it might be misplaced at that stage. John's teacher was quite happy with his progress generally, pointing out that John was well up to standard in other areas, particularly mathematics. Nevertheless, Mrs B and John's teacher agreed that John should take home a school reading book and that Mrs B would try and reinforce the work done in class.

This was the beginning of a very frustrating period for all concerned. Mrs B would spend a few minutes several times each day (or during the course of an evening) reading with John, but with no apparent success. John's mother recalls that although John might seem to have learned a word one day, next morning he behaved as though he had never seen it before. His parents became very worried about John's apparent inability to store 'word pictures' for any length of time. Mrs B remembers that, at this point, John was beginning to use his right hand more – for writing, drawing and other activities; she believes that he decided to imitate his friends and was not pressurised.

Eventually, continuous failure did begin to have some effect on John's personality. He became somewhat withdrawn, isolating himself from his classmates. Mr and Mrs B, John's teacher and the headteacher had many discussions about John's problems, but to little effect. On one occasion, Mrs B was invited to go into school on two afternoons a week to give John extra help with reading in the school situation. Again, there was no significant improvement and John's headteacher suggested that the local authority psychologist should be called in.

John was seven when this assessment was carried out. The psychologist stated that John was of above-average intelligence but behind with his reading.

John's parents were becoming quite desperate by that stage and, by chance, Mrs B mentioned her fears to another mother who knew of a child who had suffered from similar problems.

Then began a chain of events which finally led to the local dyslexia association referring John, who was eight by this time, to a private psychologist.

The psychologist confirmed Mrs B's intuition; namely that John was of above-average intelligence but suffering from a specific language disability. The report states:

> On the Wechsler Intelligence Test sub-test scores were done at a level corresponding to an Intelligence Quotient of 125... for purposes of comparison this is above the average for those who eventually take 'O' and 'A' levels ... From these results it is clear that he is suffering from a severe degree of specific dyslexia.

The psychologist's report also pointed out that John's span of auditory attention was particularly weak and that this led to a number of
educational problems. Among them were difficulties in concentrat-
ing on what was being said (particularly in noisy classrooms) and the
deleterious effect of weak auditory attention on reading and spelling
acquisition. It was further stated that John's orientation and sequencing skills were significantly underdeveloped and that this also
affected, among other things, his acquisition of literacy skills.

Remediation

After some discussion with the psychologist and with the co-operation of John's headteacher, Mr and Mrs B decided that John must
have some private tuition. The local dyslexia association recommended a teacher and John was taught by this specialist on two afternoons a week. Mrs B believes that this lady's expertise was
responsible for John's breakthrough. He began a structured phonic
programme which recommended the multisensory teaching
method. These techniques helped John to sort out his orientation
and sequencing problems. At the same time, the programme was
helping him to store sound/letter correspondences in a systematic
way. This structured approach to language was a completely new
experience for John.

John's first teacher retired and the present writer continued the
programme begun earlier. The transition was smooth, John continuing to make good progress. Having said that, John's reading and
spelling ages are about two years behind his chronological age and
he still has to work very hard to overcome his inherent disadvantages.

John's parents are very pleased that their persistence on their
son's behalf has been rewarded. John himself, while still preferring
the company of family to peers, seems to be a remarkably well-
adjusted young man who copes well with the wide variety of intellectual, emotional and practical manifestations of dyslexia.

Chapter 3
Activities and
strategies

Introduction

The principles of accepted learning theory inform this chapter; it seems to us that the idea of beginning with *concrete* tasks or 'set pieces' could be adapted to teach/improve some of the subskills related to language development: orientation, sequencing and recall are the main focus here.

Each of the following examples involves one or more of these skills. The activities are based on the structured, sequential and cumulative teaching principles recommended for dyslexics. However, the set pieces are not meant to be rigidly adhered to or definitive. You might adapt the principles mentioned above and invent your own activities to suit the particular pupil.

Activity 1

Use each closed doorway in the house/school as 'base'. Stand facing the closed door with the pupil by your side and remind him which are his left and right sides. Then ask him to point to the left and right sides of the doorway. Next, ask him to open the door, walk through the doorway and turn round to face the opening. Ask the pupil to point to the left and right sides of the doorway. Repeat this activity several times over a period until the pupil begins to see that the terms left and right are relative.

Activity 2

Choose three items of clothing. Place them in a line in the same order you would expect the pupil to don them when dressing. Ask the pupil to look at the items carefully and say what they are, starting with the item on the left, then the middle item and, finally, the right-hand item. Ask the pupil to close his eyes while you change the order. Finally, tell him to open his eyes and replace the items in the original order. You can increase the number of items (up to, say, a maximum of five) as his performance improves.

Activity 3 (game)

Choose a general category such as furniture, food, clothes, toys, and so on. The first player says (for example) 'I went to market and bought a table.' The second player says 'I went to market and bought a table and a chair', and so on. Each player has to recite all the items already chosen and add one of his own. The first player to forget an item loses.

Activity 4

Tell the pupil to listen carefully and then repeat what you say twice. Then give him a specific task involving orientation, memory and sequencing. For example: 'Go through the red door, then turn left, then walk six paces and turn right.' You can expand/adapt this idea, but never expect the pupil to remember a sequence you could not easily cope with yourself.

The next step is to transfer the skills learned through activities 1, 2, 3 and 4 to more demanding situations. You might try these exercises.

Exercise 1 (make several copies of this for the pupil to practise)

This exercise involves constant reorientation. The focus moves from left to right and back again, thus reproducing the reorientation demanded when reading and writing. Tell the pupil to use a coloured pencil to follow the route indicated by the dotted line and instructions.

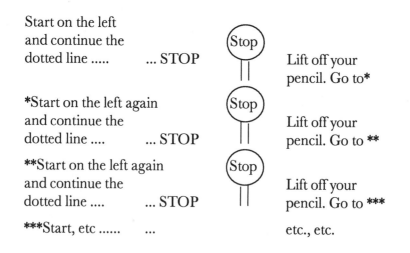

Start on the left
and continue the
dotted line .... STOP

(Stop)

Lift off your
pencil. Go to*

*Start on the left again
and continue the
dotted line .... STOP

(Stop)

Lift off your
pencil. Go to **

**Start on the left again
and continue the
dotted line .... STOP

(Stop)

Lift off your
pencil. Go to ***

***Start, etc ....

etc., etc.

Exercise 2

This is designed to improve sequencing, memory and orientation. Tell the pupil to look carefully at each of the groups below. Then cover up one group at a time and ask him to draw what he saw – in the same order. Explain that his standard of drawing and fine detail are unimportant.

(a)

(b)

(c)

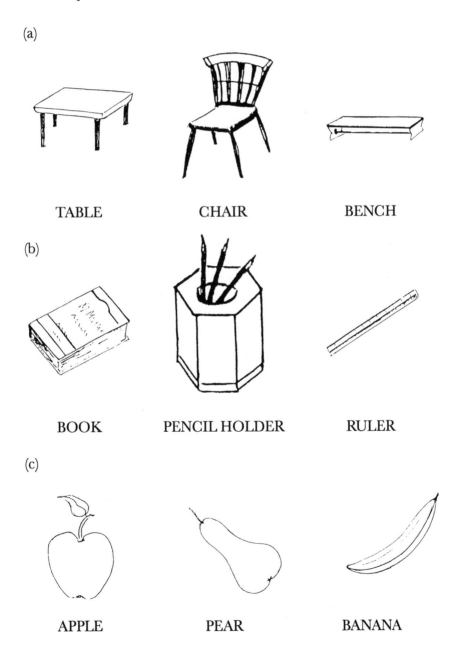

TABLE   CHAIR   BENCH

BOOK   PENCIL HOLDER   RULER

APPLE   PEAR   BANANA

Exercise 3 (if the pupil recognises and can say the names of the letters of the alphabet)

Again, this exercise is designed to improve basic subskills.

Write down and name the first three letters of the alphabet. Ask the pupil to tell you the next three. Write them down yourself or ask the pupil to write his own if he is competent to do so. Continue in this way until you reach the end of the alphabet.

Once the pupil is confident and competent at this fairly basic level, you can try the more complicated exercises which follow or move on to some of the commercial material available. The Helen Arkell Centre, for example, can supply a pack of orientation exercises, and puzzle books often include mazes, codes to be 'cracked', and so on, which are all helpful. Also, the games described at the beginning of *Alpha to Omega* can be tried at this stage.

More exercises to improve subskills

The following pictures and the questions/tasks that go with them become increasingly complex. Once more, you may care to invent supplementary reinforcing activities or build in extra exercises if you think our questions and tasks expect too much from your pupil. Again, the point to remember is that if you adopt a step-by-step approach to the exercises, the pupil is more likely to succeed. These exercises should help to solve some of the practical problems caused by poor orientation, memory and sequencing skills.

Instructions (orientation/memory/sequencing)

Remind the pupil which are his left and right sides. Put a rubber band or watch (or some other identification) on his right hand so that he has a concrete base reference. Tell him that the boys in the first five pictures also wear watches on their right hands and that his watch will be a useful 'clue'. Ask the pupil to listen carefully to the question/tasks and to repeat what you say twice. Present each picture in turn and do not articulate the next question/task until the earlier one has been dealt with.

Questions   (i)   Is this boy facing you or does he have his back to you?
             (ii)   What is the boy wearing on his right hand?
            (iii) What is the boy carrying in his left hand?

Questions (i) Is this boy facing you or does
                he have his back to you?
           (ii) What is the boy carrying in
                his right hand?
           (iii)What is the boy carrying in
                his left hand and where is his
                left leg?

Questions (i) What is the boy wearing on
                his right hand?
           (ii) What is the boy carrying in
                his left hand?

Questions (i) What is the boy carrying in
                his right hand?
           (ii) What is the boy carrying in
                his left hand and where is
                his left leg?

Questions (i) What is the boy doing with
                his right hand and which leg
                is the dog biting?
           (ii) What is the boy carrying over
                his left shoulder, and what is
                he carrying in his right hand?

Question/ (i) Which is your right eye? Now
Task   point to the man's right eye
                with your right hand.
           (ii) Which is your right eye again?
                Now point to the man's right
                eye with your left hand.

Tasks   (i) Point to this boy's right eye,
(either hand)   right hand and right leg in
                    that order.
               (ii) Point to the boy's left eye, left
                    hand and left leg in that order.
               (iii)Point to the boy's right eye
                    and then to his left hand.
               (iv) Point to the boy's left eye,
                    right and left hands in that
                    order.

Tasks (i)   Point to the person standing
               on the man's right.
       (ii)   Point to the person
               standing on the child's left.

(Tell the pupil that this is a bus station and that he should use his fingers to 'do the walking'.)

IMAGINE YOU ARE WALKING TOWARDS THE BUS STATION ENTRANCE.

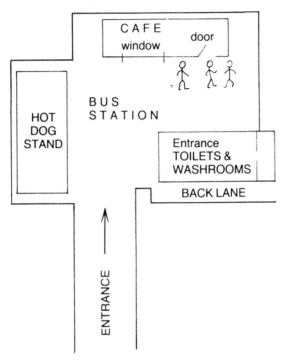

Task/Question

(i)   Go into the station and take the first left. Which building do you come to?

(ii) Go into the bus station and cross to the café. Stand facing the café door. How many people are on your right and how many people are on your left?

NOW STAND WITH YOUR BACK TO THE DOORWAY

(iii) How many people are on your right and how many people are on your left?

STAND WITH YOUR BACK AGAINST THE WINDOW OF THE CAFÉ. START TO WALK DOWN TOWARDS BACK LANE.

(iv) *Point* to the buildings on your left and then *point* to the building on your right.

(v)   *Point* to the building that is now behind you.

Conclusion

(i) Counselling, discussion and exercises will all help the dyslexic to come to terms with his motor and practical problems. Equally important, these exercises and activities are designed to cultivate those competencies (orientation, sequencing, memory) which relate to language development.

(ii) Readers investigating links between motor activities and literacy will be interested in Rob Lefoy's book, *Improving Literacy Through Motor Development*, Watford Dyslexia Unit, South Oxhey, WD1 5HA.

Chapter 4
Structure

Introduction

It is commonly agreed that the subject teacher must understand not only the *content* of his particular curriculum but also the *nature* of the discipline being taught, the ability to adapt/invent and improvise being dependent on a real grasp of the concepts involved. More specifically, teachers (and we include both paid professionals and parents here) implementing a structured phonic programme must come to terms with the concept of structure. The term carries both a general and specific definition, each being central to the real understanding of structured phonic programmes. Unfortunately, the terminology is a little obscure, but technical terms are defined and have been kept to a minimum.

(*Note*: The discussion leads on to practical 'discovery' exercises.)

Structure

The term structure might be defined, in a general way, as 'a whole – each part relating to the other' and this is a relatively apt description of the English language. Having said that, it might be more accurate to describe the mother tongue as a superstructure. This superstructure of language is, in turn, composed of other related substructures. As teachers concerned about language, we are involved with four interacting substructures which support the whole which is the English language. Those substructures are called semantic (meanings), syntactic (grammar), phonological (sounds) and graphological (written symbols). All these substructures are characterised by parts relating to the other. (Thinking of semantic substructure, for example, the word *big* is not meaningful unless we know the meaning of the word *small*.) However, while a knowledge of semantic and syntactic structures is obviously useful, the research of graphologists and phonologists is more directly related to the development of structured phonic programmes.

The phonological substructure has a limited number of parts. It is structured by 44 significant *sounds*:[1] these sounds can be manipulated to produce any word in the English language. The parts relate to each other in particular ways and have particular positions (for instance, the final sound in *sing* is always articulated after a vowel sound and is never sounded initially).

The graphological substructure also has a limited number of parts which can be organised in a variety of ways. This substructure is structured by the 26 *letters* of the Roman Alphabet. These 26 letters obviously cannot accommodate the 44 sounds in a one-to-one correspondence; the language therefore has to use a number of strategies to deal with this. For example, the language does not have one particular letter with which it can record the long medial vowel sound in *flight*.[2] thus this sound is frequently represented by the *three* letters *igh*. (There are many other instances of such strategies and these are discussed more fully in Book Three.)

The limited number of letters in the Roman Alphabet obviously makes 'spelling out the sounds' more complicated (think of the word *mechanisation*, which has 13 letters but not 13 sounds).

However, linguists have discovered that the language copes amazingly well with what is ostensibly a confusing situation. It seems that the mother tongue is approximately 90% ordered in its sound/letter correspondence; that is, certain sounds are regularly represented by combinations of letters in particular positions (think of the long medial vowel sound in *flight* again in relation to *bright, sight, night, tight,* and so on).

Discoveries like this have provided raw material for structured phonic programmes. Generally speaking, such programmes usefully take advantage of linguistic research and criteria; the material is organised into a highly effective teaching aid.

A structured phonic programme such as *Alpha to Omega* relates the parts of phonological structure to the parts of graphological structure. The term 'structure' in this context means that the 44 sounds are matched with their written form in a systematic, cumulative and cohesive teaching programme. Sound/letter correspondences are revealed progressively in such programmes. The whole programme is structured by the parts; each of these deals with a sound/letter correspondence which relates to other parts.

Structured phonic programmes therefore teach not only the one-to-one correspondence relating to the 26 letters of the Roman

Alphabet, but also the other less obvious relationships. Furthermore, because an objective of such programmes is *successful accumulation*, the pupil is never expected to deal with sound/letter correspondences he has not been specifically taught earlier. Each step in the programme is a foundation for the next level of language experience.

It will be observed that the idea of structure is central to language teaching; the concept is rooted in the linguistic theory which, implicitly and explicitly, directs structured phonic programmes. The teacher, therefore, must come to terms with both the general and specific meaning of the concept in order to take full advantage of these provenly successful teaching aids.

Discovery exercises

Introduction

To extend what has been said earlier, many teachers would accept that a deep understanding of both subject and pupil improves the quality of their teaching. It follows, therefore, that parents and teachers intending to implement a structured language programme should truly understand both the nature of language and also the nature of the pupil's difficulties. These exercises are thought to be one way of helping parents and teachers move towards that end, the general aims being as follows:

(i)   to apply and develop those principles of structure discussed earlier;

(ii)   to demonstrate the rules and regularities which exist within the language;

(iii)   to convey some idea of how it feels to be faced with more sounds than there are letters and – perhaps most important – how it feels to be faced with a completely unfamiliar recording system. (The demands made by phonemic transcription are not dissimilar to those made when a young child is first expected to write in his mother tongue.)

Discovery exercises (A)

(i to iii)

(i)   This exercise is included because the teacher/parent should appreciate how many sounds children have to discriminate, remember and organise.

Instruction. Study the list headed '44 significant sounds of English', Appendix C. Go through the list voicing each sound and illustrative word. (/æ/ as in /bæg/; /ɛ/ as in /bɛg/ and so on). Notice that there are many more sounds than letters in the English language.

(ii)   The next exercise demonstrates how highly regular the language is in its sound/letter correspondence.

Instruction. Look at the list headed '44 significant sounds of English', Appendix C. Go through the list again, this time voicing only each of the (vowel) sounds 1–18. Now try and write (say) 10 illustrative words containing the common sound for each of the vowel sounds numbered 7, 8, 15, 17 and 18.

Before beginning, note that every word in each of the five groups must contain that element which matches in terms of both sound(s) and their representation in letters. That is, an identical vowel sound must appear in each of the 10 words chosen and must be represented by the identical letter(s) each time. For instance:

/eɪ/ as in p*ay*, pl*ay*, tod*ay*, dism*ay*, and so on.

/i/ as in m*ea*n, b*ea*d, st*ea*m, and so on.

(iii) This exercise should alert teachers/parents to some of the very real difficulties confronting the less able reader/dyslexic. The teacher's experience is relative to the pupil's when he is first exposed to the 'meaningless' abstraction of letters.

Instruction. Look at the list headed '44 significant sounds of English', Appendix C. Take particular note of the *phonemic symbols*. Transcribe the following text and star (*) the transcribed symbols which are representing two or more conventional letters.

'I do think fish and chips are grand. They are cheap and fish
aɪ du θɪŋk
is very good for you. Also, you do not have to wash up if you eat them from the bag!' *Note*: Full transcription in answers (A) p. 130.

Discovery exercises (A)

(iv to vii)

The four exercises that follow provide opportunities to practise the principles of structured progressive disclosure mentioned earlier. It cannot be overemphasised that this principle is central to the successful teaching of dyslexic pupils. The authors anticipate that readers will perceive:

(1)   why it is that this tightly controlled method is most suitable for the pupil who finds language confusing;

(2)   how easy it is to make wrong assumptions about what is known; and why such false premises invite failure rather than the desired success.

(iv) *Instruction.* Assume that a pupil's work has been analysed and that he seems to know only the following:

(1)   all single consonant sound/letter correspondences of the Roman alphabet;

(2)   all short vowel sound/letter correspondences (see Appendix C);

(3)   the following *initial* consonant blends; that is, the blended consonant sounds/letters which commonly appear at the *beginning* of words: /sp/ (as in spot); /tr/ (as in trip); /dr/ (as in drop); /pl/ (as in plan); /tw/ (as in twin).

Now look at the 'Sentences for dictation' below. Put a star (*) above those initial blends that *cannot be assumed to be known.*

Sentences for dictation *

     (1) (eg) Did Gwen spit on a twig?
     (2)   Stan set a trap; Stan got a frog!
     (3)   A grub is snug in a rug.
     (4)   Did Pam put a crab on Fred's leg?
     (5)   A slim frog sat on a twig.
     (6)   Jim got a plum flan from Gran.
     (7)   Dad did not clap but Pam did.
    NB. Answers on page 130.

(v) *Instruction.* Assume that in subsequent weeks this same pupil had learned some more initial consonant blend sounds/letters, namely: /gr/ (as in grub); /kl/ (as in clap); /fr/ (as in frog); /tr/ (as in trip); and also that he now knows the following words: *the, to, and.*

Make up ten 'Sentences for dictation', remembering you can now include all the following: *sp, tr, dr, pl, tw, gr, cl, fr, the, to, and.*

Remember to check the structure of each word you choose. Are you sure the pupil is familiar with every *part* of the *whole* word?

    e.g. Grab the grub and drop it on the twig.

(vi) *Instruction.* Assume that later in the term the pupil has been taught some more sound/letter correspondences:

/ʃ/ (as in ship); /tʃ/ (as in chin); /θ/ and /ð/ (as in thin and that); /ɑ/ (as in farm).

Make up 10 'Sentences for dictation' using as many of the above as possible but excluding any parts of structure not detailed earlier in this set of exercises.

e.g. Trish and a chum got thin chips from Mark's chip shop in the park.

ASK SOMEONE TO CHECK THAT YOU HAVE NOT INCLUDED WORDS CONTAINING UNKNOWN SOUND/LETTER CORRESPONDENCES.

(vii) *Instruction.* Imagine you are teaching the same pupil (ɔ) (as in corn). Make up six 'Sentences for dictation' that include many examples of this new regularity. Remember the principle remains the same; you can only include the sound/letter correspondences and sight words listed in these exercises.

e.g. Pam got to the sports but forgot the form for the car park.

Note. Phonemic symbols are set out in the list headed '44 significant sounds of English', Appendix C.

Discovery Exercises (B)

Note. Answers on page 131.

(i)   Look at each sentence. Decide which words in the sentence contain the same sound and matching letter representation. (For instance: 'bright light', etc., in the first sentence.) List these words and say what general principle you have discovered. (For example: long /aɪ/ in the middle of a word is often represented by the three letters …)

1 It was a bright light night so we got tight and then had a fight!
2 Jean thinks meat is a treat but I scream for cream!
3 They found that the loud sound came from the Underground.
4 Today is a holiday, so we shall play and be gay.
5 You will spoil that joint if you boil it.

(ii)   (a) Underline the root in the following sentences (for instance – clap in 'clapping' in sentence (b) 1).

(b) Then work out how the addition of the suffix affects the root.

1 The audience was clapping the winning swimmer who, being thinner, was cutting through the water like a real winner.
2 We are hoping that these diving and wading exercises will result in our saving many young lives.
3 Just lately I have felt rather lonely but I have to act bravely and wisely and to be more hopeful about this tiresome problem.

Discovery exercises

Conclusion

You should now be beginning to understand both the nature of the dyslexic's problem and also the structured and regular nature of the mother tongue; it is this characteristic of the language which can be turned to the advantage of pupils who are disadvantaged linguistically.

Note. Readers who wish to pursue this topic further should see the more detailed analysis of language in Book Three.

Notes

[1]See also list headed '44 significant sounds of English' in Appendix C
[2]See also list headed '44 significant sounds of English' in Appendix C.

Chapter 5
Testing, lesson planning and record keeping

Introduction

By this stage you should be recognising some of the regular relationships between sounds and letters. You should also have begun to appreciate how a deeper understanding of language will improve teaching performance, particularly when implementing a structured phonic programme.

Another important step is deciding which of the sound/letter(s) relationships you need to teach a particular pupil. This can be a difficult decision. Analysis of the mistakes in a piece of free writing is one common way of pin-pointing difficulties but this policy has disadvantages. How do you know that there are not other more fundamental problems which have not emerged in this piece of work? What assumptions (if any) can reasonably be made? Where do you go when you have worked through your analysis? Such a piecemeal approach is beset with difficulties and permits (and even invites) the failure you wish to avoid. (The pupil who has already failed once needs to have success built in to his new learning experience.) Most importantly, a piecemeal approach is contrary to the sequential, structured and cumulative teaching envisaged by the authors of structured phonic programmes. The obvious way to ensure that no wrong assumptions are made is to start at the very beginning of a structured phonic programme; but here again there may be difficulties. The older pupil, for example, may resist the idea of working through lots of 'babyish' words with which he is already quite competent to deal.

There appears to be no perfect solution and certainly the generality of reading and spelling tests offers little help in this context. What is needed is a test that is as structured, sequential and cumulative as the structured phonic programme which is to be implemented.

The structured phonic tests printed below are directly related to the programme we decided to adopt (see 'Background and introduction'). The words selected cover all the main structures dealt with in *Alpha to Omega*. These tests are diagnostic and do not result in any hypothetical reading or spelling age; nor do they test intelligence. Of course, you could plough through *Alpha to Omega* or do random checks for yourself. However, experience has proved that pupils are easily distracted by the constant turning of pages and find the form of testing suggested here familiar and therefore less inhibiting.

You will notice that the pupil is asked only to write and not to read; spelling is being used diagnostically here. That is not to say that reading is treated as being of secondary importance. The point is that dyslexic pupils commonly have far more trouble with spelling than reading; breakdowns in sound/letter correspondence seem to occur much earlier in spelling than in reading. Generally speaking, the first breakdown in spelling will be the right point at which to start remediation. Improvement in spelling will, almost invariably, also lead to more effective decoding (reading).

Note

(i)   Pupils identified as slow learners have also been tested in this way. Such pupils have made progress when following the programme in *Alpha to Omega*, beginning at the point where the first breakdown of the sound/letter relationship occurred.

(ii)   These tests have also been used successfully in a group situation. Teachers dealing with small groups and/or remedial classes might find it convenient to test a number of pupils at the same time.

Testing: Administration – (structured phonic tests)

The test should be given in a relaxed informal atmosphere and the reasons for doing the test should be explained to the pupil. *He should write a list of the letters and words as you articulate them.* All pupils should start on Test 1. (It is amazing how many children have an unreliable grasp of short vowel sound/letter correspondences even though they know more complex sequences of sounds and letters.) The first mistake or refusal ('can't do it') should be noted, but you may care to go a little further just to check it was not a 'one-off'. If a pupil fails (through mistake or refusal) on four consecutive items, it is obviously time to stop; you have established where the first breakdown occurs.

You may repeat the test item twice but do not 'sound out' any words. However, you *may* omit any word considered to be less than meaningful to the particular pupil; another word of similar character should be substituted. (The references to *Alpha to Omega** in the far right-hand column below indicate where the appropriate word lists can be found.) Do remember this is the beginning of a new learning chapter for both you and the pupil. His motivation is more likely to be increased by a brisk 'right – now we know where to start' than by making him feel he has failed the test. He should understand that careful testing will prevent the recurrence of the failing experience with which he is all too familiar. Also, if the pupil finds the writing involved too much effort, you could break down each test into smaller units.

Note. (i) References in the far right-hand column relate to the index of *Alpha to Omega**. (ii) Phonemic symbols are set out in the list headed '44 significant sounds of English', Appendix C.

Alpha to Omega: Index Reference

Testing: Test 1   *qv*

Tester (a1)	Says the names of all the letters in the alphabet, in *random order*. Pupil writes then in 'little letters' – ie, lower case – (g, a, and so on).	(a1) Alphabet
Tester (a2)	Says the names of all the letters in the alphabet, in *random order*. Pupil writes them in 'BIG LETTERS'–ie, UPPER CASE–(T, D, and so on).	(a2) Alphabet
Tester (b1)	Says the *sounds* of all the letters in the alphabet, in *random order*. Pupil writes them in 'little letters'–ie, lower case– (b, m, and so on). *The sounds represented by letters 'c' (as in coat) and 'k' (as in king) are, of course, the same. Ask the pupil to write down both representations of this sound.	(b1) Alphabet
Tester (b2)	Says the sounds of all the letters in the alphabet, in *random order*. Pupil writes them in 'BIG LETTERS'–ie, UPPER CASE–(D, R, and so on). *See note above.	(b2) Alphabet

General note reminder

The tester articulates the sounds/words which should then be written by the pupil.

Tester (c)	Says /ʃ/ (as in shop); /tʃ/ (as in chip); /ð/ (as in that); /θ/ (as in thin)	(c) Consonant digraphs
Tester (d)	Says bat, cod, fan, gun, hat, is, jam, lid, pet, rod, van, win, box, yes, zip	(d) Vowels (short)
Tester (e)	Says shop, ship, chop, chum, that, them, thin, push, dash, rich, much, path, bath	(e) Consonant digraphs
Tester (f)	Says be, he, we, no, go, so, by, my	(f) Vowels (long)
Tester (g)	Says spot, stop, smog, snap, slip, swam, twin, plan, blot, clip, glad, flag, pram, brat, trap, drug, crab, grim, frog, dwell* * If the pupil writes 'dwel', count this as correct. You are testing consonant blends and he will be taught the 'll rule' later in the programme.	(g) Consonant blends
Tester (h)	Says desk, nest, fact, next, help, self, lift, melt, crisp	(h) Consonant blends
Tester (i)	Says sprat, split, shred, strap, scrap, thrush, squib	(i) Consonant blends
Tester (j)	Says grand, strand, spent, splint, bench, crunch, stamp, clump, sprang, string, spank, shrunk	(j) Assimilations
Tester (k)	Says landed, mended, planted, rushed, dashed, mashed	(k) Verb (past tense)
Tester (l)	Says charm, march, start, army, party, storm, north, sport, term, herb, stern	(l) ar, or, er
Tester (m)	Says want, wash, swan, squat, squash, warm, swarm, dwarf, work, worth, world	(m) W-rule I, II, III

General note reminder

The tester articulates the words which should then be written by the pupil.

Testing: Test 2

Tester (a)	Says smell, shrill, thrill	(a) -ll
Tester (b)	Says talk, chalk, walk, halt, salt	(b) -al
Tester (c)	Says class, grass, stress	(c) -ss
Tester (d)	Says grasp, flask, plaster	(d) A– 'Southern'
Tester (e)	Says staff, sniff, cliff	(e) -ff
Tester (f)	Says crack, cricket, chicken, clock	(f) -ck
Tester (g)	Says trade, scrape, stake, bathe, here, spine, grime, stripe, slope, bloke, smoke, cube, tube, plume	(g) Magic E
Tester (h)	Says love, oven, cover, above, front, dozen, month, money	(h) V, no English words ends in
Tester (i)	Says city, century, civil, citizen, circus, recent, pencil, concert, sincere, dance, pence, absence	(i) C, soft
Tester (j)	Says skill, skid, kick, kite	(j) K
Tester (k)	Says German, general, gently, giant, page, engage, exchange, village, message	(k) G, soft
Tester (l)	Says jumper, jacket, joke, just	(l) J
Tester (m)	Says guest, guide, guilt, vague, rogue	(m) gu
Tester (n)	Says edge, ledge, fridge, trudge, sludge	(n) -dge
Tester (o)	Says fetch, match, kitchen, scratch,	(o) -tch
Tester (p)	Says blind, behind, child, golden, scold, almost	(p) Vowels – long with short spellings

General reminder

The tester articulates the words which should then be written by the pupil.

Testing: Test 3

Tester (a)	Says strain, against, afraid, holiday, astray, railway	(a) ai, ay
Tester (b)	Says hair, chair, unfair, despair, repair	(b) ai
Tester (c)	Says float, groan, throat, snow, show, below	(c) oa/ow

Tester (d)	Says food, gloom, tooth, drew, flew, threw	(d) oo, -ew
Tester (e)	Says light, bright, fright, spy, cry, try	(e) igh, y
Tester (f)	Says three, agree, coffee, reach, stream, conceal	(f) ea, ee
Tester (g)	Says dread, spread, steady, wealth, health, deafen	(g) ea as /e/
Tester (h)	Says spoil, joint, poison, ointment, destroy, employ, enjoy	(h) oi, oy
Tester (i)	Says bound, ground, amount, trousers, allow, endow, growl, crowd, clown	(i) ou, ow
Tester (j)	Says because, saucer, launch, laundry, draw, claw, straw, awkward	(j) au, aw
Tester (k)	Says thirsty, first, swirl, return, church, burden, murmur, furnish, disturb	(k) ir, -ur
Tester (l)	Says learn, pearl, earth, heard, research	(l) ear as /er/

If the pupil reaches the end of Test 3 with only the occasional mistake, he is probably reasonably competent to start the suffixing rules set out in *Alpha to Omega*, Stage 3. Older pupils often are able to start at this point. Once you have established the right level by careful testing, you have largely eliminated the possibility of missing any vital structures. The time spent on testing is justified by your new awareness of the student's level of competence. All that remains is the looking-up of the breakdown point in the index of *Alpha to Omega*.

Having said that, it is as well to remember that some dyslexics spell reasonably well when all their attention is directed to the task in hand – in this instance, the diagnostic spelling test.

If there is any evidence that the pupil is 'overperforming', the first few lessons might be spent on 'revision' of earlier test items.

Finally, it is worth mentioning that feedback from many Special Needs Teams has been very positive. Indeed, the need for this type of diagnostic, programme-related test appears to be greater than it was when this book was first published.

Lesson planning

Careful lesson planning is central to all good teaching and it is particularly important when teaching the dyslexic pupil. Both teacher and pupil need to know precisely what they are doing and why. It is suggested that initially both plan and timing are actually written out, though clearly a degree of flexibility is not discouraged.

The lesson plans set out after this preamble include some description of both method and content, although obviously the former can be taken as read once a routine is established. The reader is also advised to look at the suggested lesson plan and drills (for teaching sound/letter association and dictation) set out in *Alpha to Omega*. The practice of the multisensory principles is incorporated in the Drill and further information is given in Book Two Chapter 1, Q/A 19.

To return to the particular, the plan for John B (see below) is included because it contains examples of 'original' sentences not set out in the *Alpha to Omega* programme. Teachers and parents new to the concept of structure (the notion that each part relates to the other) should be moving towards a position where they too can produce such additional material. Both parties are asked to take special note of the principle of a *structured, progressive and cumulative disclosure*.

One of the main implications of this principle is that the pupil must not be asked to write a sound/letter correspondence unless: *either* it has been specifically taught *or* the test results indicate that he knows it.

For example, John B (see below) cannot be expected to write the following sentence:

Did my Dad put on the light?

This sentence would not be used because the Case Note (see below) dictates otherwise. That is, there is *no evidence* that John B has been specifically taught the sound/letter correspondence in the middle of *light, nor* do the test results suggest he knows it.

Therefore, although we can assume (from the test results) that John would know all the other sound/letter correspondences in this sentence, *he cannot be expected to write it.* He could, on the other hand, be asked to write:

Did my Dad get in the bath?

A grasp of the principle of structured, progressive and cumulative disclosure is vital to the success of a language programme.

Finally, the reader is asked to notice that reinforcement of sound/letter correspondences dealt with in earlier lessons takes up a substantial amount of time in the examples given; in a 45-minute lesson, both John B and Michael L spend 10 minutes on this activity. Again, this is an important procedure, experience confirming that time spent in this way improves both recall and speed of response to material already taught.

John B

Case note. Breakdown occurred at item (g) Test 1. This means we can reasonably assume that John B knows all single sound/letter correspondences; also that he has learned /ʃ/ (as in ship); /tʃ/ (as in chum); /θ/ and /ð/ (as in thin and them) and the monosyllabic words, be, he, we, no, go, so, by and my. Two lessons subsequent to the test dealt with /sp/ (as in spot) and /st/ (as in stop). *No other assumptions can be made.*

Lesson 3: Plan

REVISION

(a) Ten minutes' dictation, pupil reading each word aloud as he writes it and then reading word again when he has finished writing.

Words used: shop, ship, push, dash, rush, chip, rich, chap, be, he, my, by, spit, spot, spin, span, spat, stop, step, past, fist, stub, stun.

(Notice: the pupil is asked only to deal with those sound/letter correspondences assumed to be known.)

NEW
ITEM

(b) Ten minutes to teach new sound/letters correspondence: /sm/ (as in smug). Use 'Drill for teaching letter/sound association', *Alpha to Omega*, the pupil building the sounds as he makes the word.

Dictation of words – (drill as in (a)).

Words used: smug, smog, smut.

(c) Ten minutes for dictation of sentences which incorporate only those sound/letter correspondences assumed to be known. (See also 'Drill for sentence dictation' in *Alpha to Omega*.)

CUMULATIVE
REVIEW

Sentences used:

Dad had a smut of smog on his leg.

Rush to the chip shop and get the fish and chips.

Stan has got a lot of chips; he is so smug.

Did Stan spot the smut on the dish of spam and chips?

That thin lad had a red spot on his chin.

(d) *Five minutes for pupil* to read a very simple reader.

(e) Five minutes for teacher to read to pupil from a book of appropriate interest level.

(f) *Possible addition.* A commercial game or a home-made one (see Chapter 6).

Note. Phonemic symbols are set out in the list headed '44 Significant Sounds of English', Appendix C.

Michael L

Case note. Breakdown occurred at item (n) Test 2. We can reasonably assume that Michael L knows all sound/letter correspondences listed prior to item (n) in Test 2. Four lessons subsequent to the test dealt with

/dʒ/ (as represented in words like bri*dge*, fri*dge*, fu*dge*, etc);
/tʃ/ (as represented in words like ca*tch*, sna*tch*, fe*tch*, etc);
/aɪ/ (as represented in words like k*i*nd, bl*i*nd, ch*i*ld, etc);
/əʊ/ (as represented in words like g*o*ld, c*o*ld, m*o*st, etc).

No other assumptions can be made.

Lesson 4: Plan

REVISION

(a) Ten minutes' dictation, pupil reading each word aloud as he writes it and then reading word again when he has finished writing.

Words used: bridge, fudge, badge, badger, midge, midget, dodge, fetch, catch, match, kitchen, butcher, blind, kind, behind, find, most, almost, cold, bold, sold.

(*Notice*: the pupil is asked only to deal with those sound/letter correspondences assumed to be known.)

NEW
ITEM

(b) Fifteen minutes to teach new sound/letter correspondence /eɪ/ (as represented in words like tr*ai*n, br*ai*n, f*ai*nt, etc) commonly appearing in the centre of a word.

Use 'Drill for teaching letter/sound association'– *Alpha to Omega*. Pupil then makes words listed in *Alpha to Omega*, using letter box and building the sounds as he makes the word.

Dictation of same words.

(Drill as in 'John B' (a).)

CUMULATIVE
REVIEW

(c) Ten minutes for dictation of some of the sentences set out in *Alpha to Omega*. (See also 'Drill for sentence dictation' in *Alpha to Omega*.) Alternatively, 'original sentences *(including only the sound / letter correspondences listed prior to item (n) Test 2 and those specifically taught since)* could be dictated.

(d) Five minutes for pupil to read a very simple reader.

(e) Five minutes for teacher to read to pupil from a book of appropriate interest level.

(f) *Possible addition.* A commercial game or a home-made one (see Chapter 6).

Note. Phonemic symbols are set out in the list headed '44 Significant Sounds of English', Appendix C.

Record Keeping

The beauty of following a cumulative structured phonic programme is that record keeping is virtually eliminated on two counts.

First, the authors of the programme continue to include sound/letter correspondences already taught as the programme progresses; if an odd sound/letter correspondence has been forgotten, it will emerge quite naturally. The 'breakdown' can be dealt with immediately and, generally speaking, this eliminates the need for carrying forward notes. Second, if the teacher wishes to produce an independent record of the work covered, for some reason, she merely has to note the sound/symbol correspondences covered in the programme to date.

Irregular words such as *water, some,* and so forth may be the exception here and it is perhaps worth making a separate list in order to keep a check on these. It is suggested that initially this list comprise only two or three irregular words, new items being added as required. Again, the teacher's expectations here should not be overambitious. It is truly difficult for a dyslexic to learn many of the irregular words in the language. A long spelling list of such words – precipitately given – would inevitably be counter-productive.

Chapter 6
Games

Introduction

Traditional educationists might argue that word games merely add variety to language programmes, but experience suggests that games may also make a fundamental and real contribution to reading and spelling development.

Many educationists would agree that the dyslexic pupil, in particular, needs the reinforcement of regular and related language activity. However, even when reading matter (for example) is carefully graded, extra reading lessons can be a wearing experience for both teacher and pupil. By contrast, games by their very nature inspire a more light-hearted approach, helping to break down the emotional barriers which inhibit both learning and teaching.

Of course, games for dyslexics must be as carefully *structured* as reading programmes if they are to be totally successful. Also, bearing in mind the principles discussed earlier, they should provide opportunities for massive reinforcement of particular sound(s)/letter(s) correspondences; such opportunities obviously help to promote long-term storage and improve recall. It is hoped that parents and teachers will develop their own ideas from these games, perhaps using the basic formats as models. 'Other useful ideas' and 'Examples of word search activities' are appended after 'Games'. It is hoped that these examples, too, will be similarly adapted according to the sound/letter correspondence being taught.

Note. Younger children have been found to benefit from the *Lyn Wendon Pictogram System*. This system links each letter to a character (an animal or a person), the accompanying stories having a clear appeal for the young imagination.

Game I

Aim

To reinforce associations between long vowel sounds and spelling patterns

Requirements

58 pieces of blank card (say 5 cm x 5 cm)
4 different coloured pencils plus a black pencil

Construction

Divide the cards into four sets of 13 and one set of 6.
Mark a big black star in the middle of each of the six cards.
Using the black pencil to write the 'framing' letters, make a card for each word, writing the significant letter(s) in a contrasting colour.*
Thus:

RED   p ai d   tr ai n   dism ay   str ay   fr ee   thr ee

             st ea m   fl oa t   elb ow   f oo d   scr ew   br igh t   sh y

GREEN   cr ea m   c oa t   sn ow   p oo l   thr ew   l igh t

             wh y   br ai n   pl ay   tr ee   ch ea p   thr oa t   cr ow

BLUE   sch oo l   dr ew   fl igh t   fl y   ag ai n   aw ay

             coff ee   pl ea se   r oa d   gr ow   st oo l   ch ew   n igh t

ORANGE   tr y   dr y   afr ai d   holid ay   agr ee   r ea ch   dr ea m

             st ea l   s oa p   sl ow   t oo th   st ew   t igh t

The basic principles of the game can be adapted to suit the individual pupil, easier or more difficult words being substituted according to ability. This game is best played by two people, but can accommodate more.

*Note: (single lines) beneath letter(s) = write letter(s) in RED
         (two lines) beneath letter(s) = write letter(s) in GREEN
         (three lines) beneath letter(s) = write letter(s) in BLUE
         (four lines) beneath letter(s) = write letter(s) in ORANGE

Instructions for playing

The pack is shuffled and then each of the two players is dealt seven cards. The fifteenth card is placed word side up next to the pack, which is placed the opposite way. The first player has to *match* either the *colour* or the significant letter *pattern* of the turned-up card. Thus, he can place (for example, c oa t on top of r oa d, or fl igh t on top of r oa d. If he cannot go, he picks up an unknown card from the pack. Playing or picking up a card constitutes one turn. The next player repeats his procedure by matching (by colour or pattern) the last card played. If a player has a 'starred' card, he can play it as his turn directing 'change colour to ____'. The first player to get rid of all his cards wins.[1]

Games II–V: Snakes and Ladders

Aims

Each of these games is designed to teach/reinforce a particular sound/spelling pattern as follows:

Game II	deals with single consonant/short vowel/single consonant pattern (see p. 115).
Game III	deals with initial consonant blend/short vowel/final consonant patterns (see p. 116).
Game IV	deals with the effect of w on the vowel sound following (see p. 117).
Game V	deals with the effect of e, i and y on g (see p. 118).

Requirements, construction and general instructions

Large piece of card (say 30 cm x 20 cm) and coloured pencils.
Copy or trace from the following pages the game selected, introducing colours to give an attractive, interesting appearance.
All these games follow a 'Snakes and Ladders' principle. Each game could be played by several players but it is probably most effective when played by the pupil and teacher. Each player needs a counter, (a button will do), pencil and pad. A die and egg-cup are also required.

Instructions for playing

1 The pupil shakes the die first and counts off the boxes (☐) according to the number shaken. For example: if in Game II, the pupil shakes a '4', he will land on the fourth box (d-t). He then

---

[1]The game is based on the principles of 'Rummy', colour matching increasing the player's opportunities to dispose of his cards.

has to decide on a sensible word which fits the requirements outlined in the box–he would choose *dot* in this instance.

2   He then has to write his word, sounding it as he does so.

3   Instructions regarding the symbols entered in the boxes ($\boxed{*}$ $\boxed{\angle}$) vary but are noted on the individual sheets below.

4   Also, the arrows on the snakes and/or on the ladders indicate moves upwards and downwards and two words have to be written when these routes are followed.

5   If the pupil cannot say the word, being unable to work out what it would be, or writes it wrongly, he forfeits his next turn.

6   The teacher then shakes the die and repeats the pupil's actions. She writes her own word. (Thus, the pupil is not overburdened with writing and is free to anticipate future moves: 'How far away are the ladders?' 'Which words shall I have ready in case I need them?', and so on.)

Note. The basic principles of these games can be adapted to teach/reinforce many other sound/letter patterns. Also, the instruction to write the words can be ignored if the teacher believes this would be too much for the pupil. In that event, the players would build and then say the whole word but refrain from writing.

Game II

Make a sensible word by picking any one of the short vowel sounds (

(ă, ĕ, ĭ, ŏ, ŭ)

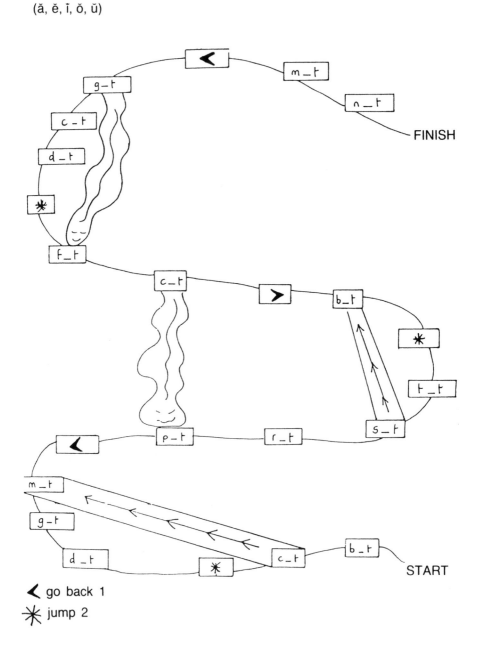

FINISH

START

❮ go back 1

✳ jump 2

Game III

Make a sensible word by picking any one of the short vowel sounds (

(ă, ĕ, ĭ, ŏ, ŭ)

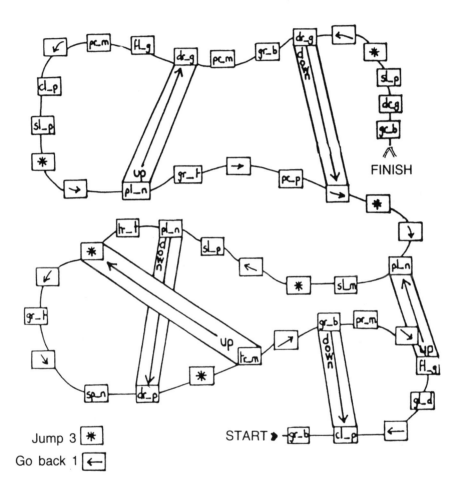

Jump 3 [✳]

Go back 1 [←]

Game IV

Add wa What's your word?

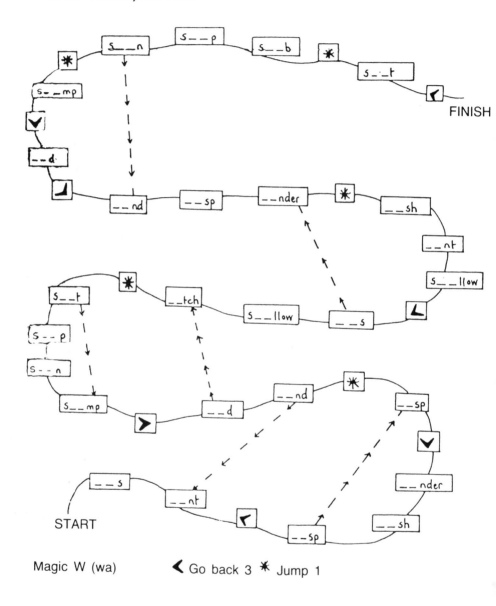

Magic W (wa)   ❮ Go back 3 ＊ Jump 1

Game V

Soft g: is it ge, gi or gy?

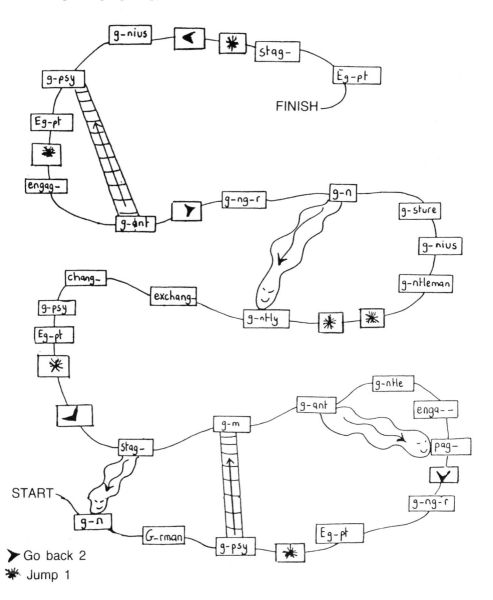

➤ Go back 2
✳ Jump 1

Games VI and VII

Games VI and VII are examples of a very flexible and useful type of track game: a basic board allows a number of variations.

Game VI: Snooker

Aim

Revision/reinforcement of a selected range of sound/letter correspondences.
(This game is probably most effective when played by the pupil and his teacher, but it could be adapted to accommodate a number of players.)

Requirements

Piece of green card (say 30 cm x 20 cm), covered with Tackyback.
10 large red counters
 2 large pink counters
 1 large brown counter
 1 large green counter
 1 large yellow counter
 1 large blue counter
 1 large black counter

List* of, say, 50 words (prepared by teacher) covering selection of sound/letter correspondences taught to date, irregular words or whatever revision is appropriate.

Construction

See illustration; using Tipp-Ex, mark the counters as follows:
red counter = 1
pink counter = 6
brown counter = 4
green counter = 3
yellow counter = 2
blue counter = 5
black counter = 7

Game VI: Snooker

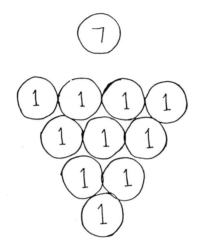

Using Blu-Tack, attach the numbered counters to the green card. Analyse the word list and grade/score each word from 1 to 7, according to the perceived degree of difficulty. (A higher grade/score of 7 relates to the most difficult words whilst a grade/score of 1 pertains to (say) simple cvc words–*cat, man* and so forth.)

Instructions for playing

The game follows (loosely) the rules of snooker (as seen on TV), but it can also be adapted in a number of different ways to suit individual circumstances/pupils.

Basically, the pupil decides which counter he intends/hopes to remove from the board. He might, for instance, choose to begin with relatively easy words (red counters, graded/scored 1).

In this case, the teacher asks him to write a word from the word list which has been given a grade/score of 1.

If the pupil writes the word correctly, he removes a red counter, records his cumulative score (1) and decides which counter he intends/hopes to remove next. The basic procedure described above is then repeated.

If he cannot spell the word/writes it incorrectly, this counts as his 'break' (to use the terminology of snooker).

Experience suggests that pupils quickly grasp the rules and objectives of this popular game.

Game VII Track and Tack

Aim

Revision/reinforcement of a particular sound/letter correspondence (spelling)

Requirements, construction and general instructions

Piece of card (say 30 cm x 20 cm)
Coloured felt-tip pens
40 small cards (say 8 cm x 5 cm)
From the illustration, copy or trace the game introducing colours to give an attractive appearance.
Take 20 small cards and mark one side of each with a triangle (Δ). (Stick-on shapes look good, but are not essential.)
These are the *instruction cards* and the reverse of each one should give an *instruction*, as follows:

5 cards to be marked JUMP 4

5 cards to be marked JUMP 2

5 cards to be marked GO BACK 2

5 cards to be marked GO BACK 4

This set of instruction cards should be shuffled prior to play.

Take the remaining 20 cards and mark one side of each with a circle (O).

Game VII

1 △	2 △	3 ○	4 ○	5 △	6 △	7 ○	8 ○	9 △	10 ○
11 △	12 ○	13 ○	14 △	15 △	16 ○	17 △	18 ○	19 ○	20 ○
21 △	22 ○	23 △	24 △	25 ○	26 ○	27 △	28 ○	29 ○	30 △
31 ○	32 △	33 ○	34 ○	35 ○	36 △	37 ○	38 △	39 △	40 ○
41 ○	42 ○	43 △	44 ○	45 △	46 ○	47 △	48 ○	49 ○	50 △
51 ○	52 △	53 ○	54 △	55 △	56 ○	57 ○	58 △	59 ○	60 △
61 ○	62 △	63 ○	64 △	65 △	66 ○	67 ○	68 ○	69 ○	70 ○

These are the *spelling cards*. On the reverse of each write a word from the selected word family. (The oa family might, for example, include: *oat, boat, coat, float, goat, throat, load, road, toad, coal, foal, goal, loaf, moan, groan, loan, oak, soak, soap and oath.*)

This game is, in many ways, a typical board game. It could be played by many players but is most effective when played by the pupil and teacher. Each player needs a counter (a button will do), pencil and pad. A die and egg-cup are also required.

Instructions for playing

1   The pupil shakes the die first and counts off the squares according to the number shaken.
2   If he lands on a square showing a triangle (Δ), he picks up an *instruction card*, reads it and obeys the instruction – JUMP 4, or whatever.
3   If he lands on a square showing a circle (O), the teacher picks up a *spelling card* and says the word which the pupil then attempts to write.
4   If the pupil cannot write the word correctly, he forfeits his next turn.
5   The teacher then shakes the die and the game continues on these lines.

Note: The basic board and *instruction cards* can be used time and time again. The *spelling cards* can be changed to suit the particular focus/object. Having said that, old *spelling cards* are worth keeping for revision purposes.

Game VIII: Snap

Aim

To improve response to any 6 irregular words.

Requirements

48 pieces of blank card and approximately 8 cm x 5 cm, and coloured pencils.

Construction

Divide the cards into 6 sets of 8. Write the same word on every card in the set. (For example – 8 × sword; 8 × store; 8 × water; 8 × forward; 8 × door; 8 × poor.)

Instructions for playing

Exactly as for the common 'Snap' game, except that the player must also say each word as he plays it. The first player to say a matched word followed by 'snap' wins all the cards already played.

Note: Any set of 'difficult' words could be substituted. For example, words containing as yet unknown spelling patterns which appear in the child's reading book or a set of 'social signs' (Private, Danger, Toilet, and so on). The cards can be 'cut down' to use again and/or one card from each set retained as part of a 'flash card revision pack'.

Game IX (Revision)

Aim

To reinforce a wide variety of sound/symbol correspondences in their permitted/likely positions. ('ng' in a triangle for example ($\triangle$) – indicates that this word *ending* is required.)

Requirements and construction

Large pieces of card (say 60 cm x 20 cm) and coloured pencils. Copy or trace Game IX (Appendix D) onto the card introducing colours to give an attractive, interesting impression.

Instructions for playing

This game could be played by several players, but is probably most effective when played by teacher and pupil. Each player needs a counter, pencil and pad. A die and egg-cup are also required.

The pupil shakes the die and counts off each shape.

for example, would each count as one shape, a throw of six bringing the player to (($\rightarrow$)). In this instance, he would 'go back four'. If he lands on (✿) he must 'jump five'. When he lands on a shape containing letters, he must think of a word which contains these letters in the position indicated. The pupil should be encouraged to 'talk himself through' the activity, thus: 'The triangle in a circle (ie) means it is a middle or an end of a word, so I could have chief or pie.' He must then write his word, sounding it out as he does so. If he cannot think of a word or spells it wrongly, he forfeits his next turn.

The teacher then shakes the die and repeats the player's actions. She writes her own word. (Thus the pupil is not overburdened with writing and is free to anticipate future moves: 'How far away are the ladders?': 'which words shall I have ready in case I need them?', and so on. The arrows indicate moves upwards and downwards and two words have to be written when these routes are followed.

Alternate moves are made until one of the players wins by passing FINISH.

Note. This game as illustrated is only suitable for the dyslexic who is well advanced in his language programme.

Other useful ideas

Many pupils appear to develop easy and effective ways of dealing with difficult words, inventing highly individual mnemonics and cues to compensate for any weaknesses. Dyslexic pupils – maybe because inherent reading and/or spelling organisational difficulties over-whelm them – seem less inclined to do this but can often be directed to 'discover' such strategies.

Of course, the efficacy of mnemonics, rhymes, and so on ('When two vowels go out walking the first vowel does the talking') is familiar to most teachers; various such examples appear in phonic structured programmes and other language development schemes. However, the aim here is not to provide a compendium of established and well-documented ideas, but to give examples of the kind of thing which can be invented both by and for the individual pupil. All the ideas which follow have been used by the present writer; it is hoped that teachers might use them as a basis for the development of other teaching aids.

Sentences

OU
'<u>O</u>, <u>U</u> y<u>ou</u>ng men sh<u>ou</u>ld visit all the c<u>ou</u>ntry pubs; I w<u>ou</u>ld if I c<u>ou</u>ld. I sh<u>ou</u>ld drink d<u>ou</u>bles and get into tr<u>ou</u>ble.'
<u>OULD</u> (c<u>ould</u>, w<u>ould</u>, sh<u>ould</u>)
'<u>O</u>, <u>U</u> lovely <u>d</u>uck!'
IR/ER/UR: which one? The associations in a 'silly sentence' assists recall:
'On the f<u>ir</u>st of the th<u>ir</u>d, I washed th<u>ir</u>ty d<u>ir</u>ty sk<u>ir</u>ts and sh<u>ir</u>ts because of the d<u>ir</u>ty b<u>ir</u>ds.'

'E got on my sister's nerves when he served all those herbs last term.'

'U made a purple burn on my arm on Thursday. it hurt so I turned to the nurse.'

AI/EA/IGH/OA/OO

'The rain in Spain was a pain when it burst the main drain and flooded the train.'

'Steamed meat is a treat but heated cream is a dream.'

'What a sight last night when he ended the fight with that frightful right.'

'Don't boast about the roast, tomorrow it's toast.'

Examples of mnemonics devised by the author's pupils

YACHT
Yachts and canoes hunt tuna.

SUGAR
Sugar upsets gulls and robins.

MANY
Many animals notice youngsters.

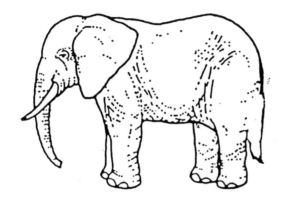

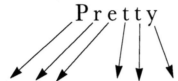

Pretty red elephant's tail turns yellow.

Colour the picture.

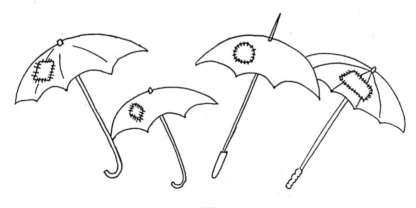

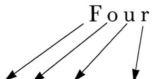

Four orange umbrellas repaired.

Colour the picture.

Word search: a

A *Find*: cat, mat, sat, rat, hat, bad, lad, sad

```
l  a  d  b  e  f  g  h  i  q  r
l  m  i  c  j  k  s  a  d  t  u
n  k  f  d  g  h  o  p  s  d  e
j  h  i  j  h  a  t  b  v  c  z
b  a  d  k  l  m  n  y  r  a  t
f  g  d  x  l  m  o  w  t  w  x
e  c  z  m  a  t  n  o  s  b  y
c  a  t  p  q  s  a  t  r  u  v
```

B *Say*: cat, mat, sat, rat, hat, bad, lad, sad

C *Write*: cat, mat, sat, rat, hat, bad, lad, sad

Word search: e

A *Find*: get, let, met, net, pet, set, wet, leg, beg

```
a  k  j  i  f  d  m  m  e  t  n
g  e  t  b  c  s  t  u  n  e  t
b  g  h  l  e  t  p  v  l  m  o
c  a  z  q  r  x  w  p  e  t  k
d  g  h  i  y  s  e  t  j  i  g
f  w  e  t  r  z  y  x  b  e  g
j  n  k  l  l  e  g  a  b  c  d
q  o  p  m  s  t  w  u  v  f  h
```

B *Say*: get, let, met, net, pet, set, wet, leg, beg

C *Write*: get, let, met, net, pet, set, wet, leg, beg

Word search: i

A *Find*: hid, lid, tip, hit, sit, lit, bit, fit, pit

j	i	g	x	f	i	t	f	a	z	x
b	i	t	f	h	m	y	e	h	i	t
z	a	b	e	w	l	i	t	y	w	p
d	o	c	p	i	t	m	g	b	u	q
p	q	n	t	d	v	g	h	m	t	v
s	s	i	t	u	c	t	i	p	n	o
r	b	c	f	h	i	d	h	l	i	d
a	d	e	j	k	l	l	j	k	s	r

B *Say*: hid, lid, tip, hit, sit, lit, bit, fit, pit

C *Write*: hid, lid, tip, hit, sit, lit, bit, fit, pit

Word search: o

A *Find*: dog, log, cot, hot, not, lot, dot, got, pot

d	o	g	b	v	d	x	u	l	f	z
h	g	e	y	l	o	g	x	g	e	a
i	w	f	c	j	k	y	c	o	t	c
j	a	l	m	h	o	t	h	v	b	d
z	n	o	t	s	t	j	k	l	m	n
n	o	p	h	i	l	o	t	d	o	t
r	q	g	o	t	c	u	s	w	p	q
a	b	q	f	d	e	t	p	o	t	r

A *Say*: dog, log, cot, hot, not, lot, dot, got, pot

C *Write*: dog, log, cot, hot, not, lot, dot, got, pot

Word search: u

A *Find*: cut, hut, nut, put, cub, pub, tub, bun, run

a	b	c	c	u	t	n	l	m	y	u
r	u	n	d	e	f	h	u	t	x	v
d	b	a	n	u	t	g	k	w	j	z
b	u	n	z	r	h	i	p	u	t	s
y	c	c	u	b	o	j	b	a	k	r
e	t	v	q	s	p	p	u	b	l	e
i	w	t	u	b	q	o	i	m	d	t
h	f	x	j	g	p	h	n	c	g	f

B *Say*: cut, hut, nut, put, cub, pub, tub, bun, run

C *Write*: cut, hut, nut, put, cub, pub, tub, bun, run

Discovery exercises: answers (A)

I do think fish and chips are
(aɪ du θɪŋk fɪʃ ænd tʃɪps ɑ)
grand. They are cheap and fish
(grænd ðeɪ ɑ tʃip ænd fɪʃ)
is very good for you. Also you
(ɪz verɪ gʊd fɔ jʊ ɔlsəʊ jʊ)
do not have to wash up if
(dʊ nɒt hæv tʊ wɒʃ ʊp ɪf)
you eat them from the bag!
(jʊ it ðem frɒm ðə bæg)

Discovery exercises: answers (A)

1 Did Gwen spit on a twig?
2 Stan set a trap, Stan got a frog!
3 A grub is snug in a rug.
3 Did Pam put a crab on Fred's leg?
5 A slim frog sat on a twig.
6 Jim got a plum flan from Gran.
8 Dad did not clap but Pam did.

Discovery exercises: answers (B)

A   1 bright, light, night, tight, fight
       long /aɪ/ sound in a medial position is often represented by
       igh.
    2 Jean, meat, treat, scream, cream
       Long /i/ sound in the medial position is often represented
       by *ea*.
    3 found, loud, sound, Underground
       Long /aʊ/ sound in the medial position is often represented
       by *ou*.
    4 today, holiday, play, gay
       Long /eɪ/ sound finally is often represented by *ay*.
    5 spoil, joint, boil
       Long /ɔɪ/ sound in the medial position is often represented
       by *oi*.

B   1 clap, win, swim, thin, cut, win
       When a word has one short vowel before a single final
       consonant, double that consonant before adding the ending.
    2 hope, dive, wade, save
       When a word ends in 'lazy e', drop it before adding the
       ending, *if that ending begins with a vowel*.
    3 late, lone, brave, wise, hope, tire
       When the ending begins with a consonant, keep the 'lazy e'
       and just add the ending.

'Readers perceive in various ways as their purpose may
     best be attained'.
Cited by E.B. Huey in *The Psychology and Pedagogy of Reading*, 1908, p.
102

'The system works by providing meaning and sound information
in a manner efficient for the judiciously sampling and constructing
reader.'
L.R. Gleitman and P. Rozin, 1977

'...a host of processes acting in concert...'
L.C. Ehri in Snowling and Thomson, 1991

Book Three
Information: reading and the English writing system

Chapter 1
The English writing system: monosyllables

Basics of the Reading Process; Scanning the Lines

Reading is the act of decoding written or printed *\<words\>* so as to arrive at their meaning.

Therefore the writing system takes great care to make words visually distinct and easily recognisable: every word is given its own special 'spelling' which never changes.

However, fluent readers do not 'sound out' or otherwise analyse a text *word by word*. Instead, they scan the lines in a rapid and complex way which allows them at any given moment to be

> interpreting the current text
> reviewing what has gone before
> building up an impression of what is to come (Figure 17).

Sifting the Information

Linked to, and interwoven with, the complex visual process of optical scanning there is an equally complex mental process, best described as 'probing guess work', which gathers, sifts and co-ordinates the four different kinds of information carried by *\<words\>*, namely

> phonic information
> graphic information
> semantic information
> syntactic information

The four types are explained and discussed below.

Beginning readers operate the same process of scanning and sifting

137

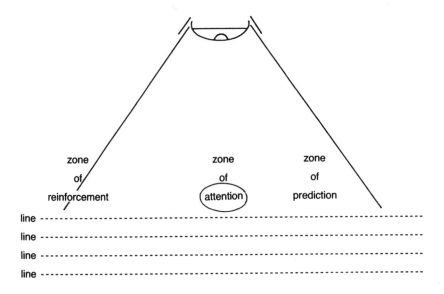

Figure 17. Optics of the reading process.

as fluent readers do, but far less efficiently. Their reading improves as their guesswork improves.

The writing system is designed for fast reading and is functional for that purpose.

Most children develop fluent reading through a reasonably smooth educational process but there are some for whom the acquisition of fast reading is hindered or blocked by barriers or resistances that may be social, psychological or linguistic.

These impediments usually occur together, but are blended in different proportions according to the nature of the individual situation. With dyslexics it is linguistic difficulties which predominate. (See introduction, p. xii and footnote 2.)

The Linguistics of the Reading Process

Written words carry four kinds of information which are 'read off' simultaneously and very efficiently in the decoding process:

1. Phonic information

Written <*words*> represent the *sounds*[1] of corresponding spoken /words/, (<sit> represents /sɪt/)
This aids *reconstruction*.

2 Graphic information

Words have characteristic and individual *designs*
(<ruff> has a different shape from <rough>) [2]
This aids *recognition*.

3 Semantic information

Words have *meaning*. ('The shot missed the t—g-t')
This aids *contextualisation*.[3]

4 Syntactic information

Words have *grammatical potential*.
('a - - - of - - -' permits 'a want of sense' but precludes 'a went of
since'.) This aids *prediction* (see Book, Ch. 3)
   The teaching of reading has been dominated by schools of
thought which have each tended to emphasise the importance of one
kind of information while devaluing the others. In fact, all four
modes.

>   phonic
>   graphic
>   semantic
>   syntactic

are of equal importance for fluent reading.

The Phonic Approach

However, the first or phonic function is *primary* in two senses:
a. It provides the foundation for all the others. The arrangement of
letters which gives to each word its characteristic pattern is not
arrived at by accident but expresses a relationship between the letters
of the alphabet and the sounds of spoken language. <*kettle*> and
<*bottle*> share some of the same letters because /kɛtl̩/ and /bɒtl̩/
share some of the same sounds. So if we decide to invent a new word
like *brilk* (/brɪlk/), the rules of alphabetic writing will decide more or
less how the new word should be written down so that other people
can read it. In the same way, when Jonathan Swift coined the names
'Lilliput' and 'Struldbrugg' for *Gulliver's Travels*, the sounds of the new
words dictated their shapes and the shapes then conveyed their
sounds.
   It is probable that when we are reading at speed (and it must
always be remembered that the writing system is designed for fluent

reading), the sound impression of the written word is much subordi-
nated to its visual impact. Nevertheless, the sound impression is
always latently present and available for reference. The silent reading of verse, for instance, would be laborious or impossible if the
printed word were not 'heard' at some level. ('The simple fact is that
the inner saying or hearing of what is read seems to be the core of
ordinary reading: the "thing in itself",' Huey, 1908, p. 102.)
b. The phonic function is also primary in the sense that it forms
the natural starting point for the *teaching of reading*. Attempts to
dispense with the 'sounds' and even the names of the letters have
generally been unavailing and have not led to quicker or more intelligent learning; it seems clear that the writing system itself offers the
most logical way into written language, the names of the letters leading into their sounds and the sounds leading into the structure of the
word. There is no good reason to reject this well-trodden path.[4, 5]

It is, of course, true that a phonic strategy will not by itself enable a
reader to identify words quickly and accurately, but nor will any other:
a combined assault is always necessary. The point being made here is
that the phonic strategy *permits and underlies* the others. It is also the one
that works best with dyslexics of all ages since it makes the least
demand on memory and on linguistic intuition. However, recognition
of the primacy of phonic strategy *does not* imply any devaluation of the
others. It cannot be stated too often that all four have to be employed
simultaneously for effective reading. Readers make continuous use of

> sounds *and*
> shapes *and*
> meanings *and*
> syntactic structures.

It follows from all this that words should, as far as possible, be read in
context and not in isolation.

Problems of the English Writing System

A perfectly 'phonic' writing system would behave like the phonemic
alphabet set out in Appendix C. (See below, *Phoneme and Grapheme*,
p. 140, for further discussion.) In such a system

> there is one letter to go with each sound of the spoken
> language;
> the same sound is always represented by the same letter
> the same letter;
> the same letter always stands for the same sound.

So, for instance, the sounds /æ/ /m/ and /d/ are consistently (and 'phonically' represented in the words <mad> and <dam>:

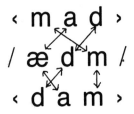

In the English writing system, the normal state of affairs is, as is well known, far otherwise; it is common to find the same *sound* represented in several different ways, as, for instance, the sound /eɪ/ in

r <u>eig</u> n
r <u>ei</u> n
r <u>ai</u> n
str <u>aigh</u> t
g <u>a</u> t <u>e</u>

and the same *letter* standing for several different sounds like the letter <*o*> in

one (/wʌ n/)
woman (/w ʊ mən/)
women (/w ɪ mɪn/)
body (/b ɒ dɪ/)
bone (/b əʊ n/)

Some spellings are hard to reconcile with any phonic scheme, as when the letter <u> is used to represent the sound /ɛ/ in *bury* or the letter <a> in *any, many,* moreover, sound/letter relationships vary freely from dialect to dialect. However, only a very limited amount of irregularity is tolerated *within one dialect system*. Even the outlandish *bury* is spelt 'phonically' apart from the letter <u> and therefore remains 75% 'regular'. In any case, to say that a system is not phonically *consistent* is by no means to say that it is not *phonic*. There are different ways of being phonic, rather as there are different ways of being intelligent, religious or democratic. As far as teaching is concerned, it is pointless either to pretend that the spelling system is more regular than it is, or to abandon it altogether as a stepping-stone for readers. The simpler regularities that do exist are more than sufficient to provide a point of entry and a continuing support for the beginning reader, bearing in mind:

1. that phonics is an aid to reading and not an end in itself;
2. that all beginning readers have to use phonics to some extent since the writing system is phonically determined;
3. that dyslexics continue to be heavily dependent on phonic information;
4. that all readers will supplement the phonic cues with graphic, syntactic and contextual information derived from the text.

Reading, we may remind ourselves, is the act of decoding written or printed words *so as to arrive at their meaning.*

Phoneme and Grapheme

The intention throughout this book has been to use technical terminology as little as possible. However, since both these terms crop up repeatedly in discussions and research literature, it may be helpful to consider them briefly here.

Phonemes

Speakers of *English*, for example, get along with about 44 different *sound units*, but it would not make sense to say that they use only 44 different *sounds*. Apart from the obvious truth that no two occurrences of a sound will be exactly 'the same' even in the mouth of a single speaker, it is also the case that users of the many different styles and dialects of English throughout the world will 'utter' their 44 sound units in different ways. (Consider, for instance 'Northern' and 'Southern' pronunciations of the word *love*.) It is nevertheless possible to present a complete list of the sound units needed for English speech (Appendix C provides such a list for the purposes of this book) and the members of this set of units will be what are technically known as *phonemes*; more formally, 'the exhaustive set of perceived minimal sound distinctions in a language.' The actual sounds which realise phonemes in speech are known as *phones*.

Graphemes

Having analysed the 'actual' sounds of *speech* into the more abstract units called phonemes, it then becomes reasonable to ask whether any corresponding entity exists in the *written language*, and in fact the symbols of an orthography operate precisely at this level of analysis. The orthographic forms that represent phonemes are sometimes referred to as *graphemes*. Using these terms one can capture the famous irregularity of the English orthography in the statement that the number of *graphemes* for English far exceeds the number of *phonemes* as, for instance, in the examples given in the preceding section where the five graphemes

<eig><ei><ai><aigh><a...e>

all correspond to the phoneme /*ei*/.

Hall (1960) defines *grapheme* as 'a significant unit of visually perceived form' and lists several varieties including:

single	e.g.	<a>
compound		<th>
discontinuous compound		<vowel> (<consonant>) <e>
		<i> t e>
one grapheme = two phonemes		<th> = /θ/ and /ð/
one grapheme = phoneme combination		<x> = /ks/.

Functions of an Alphabetic Writing System

Before one can reasonably assess the achievements of a writing system, it is necessary first to arrive at an understanding of its *intentions*–what it is setting out to do. Much of what at first seems to be eccentric is then seen to be understandable and even functional.

In brief, the letter shapes that go to make up an English <word> have to satisfy two requirements which are often in conflict.

> *a.* (Phonic) they have to express in some way the sounds of the corresponding spoken /word/.
> *b.* (Graphic) they have to create a unique and easily recognisable *image*.

When the two requirements come into conflict, then requirement *a* must give way to requirement *b*. In a system geared for fluent reading, the first duty of a word is to look *different from other words*.

This ordering of priorities has important consequences for English spelling and we shall now discuss these briefly before embarking on our study of the system.

To begin with, it is clear that the more letters a word has, the more opportunities it has for looking 'different'. So, in one way, it is advantageous for a word to be 'long' (have many letters): its very length makes it easy for the word to develop interesting and memorable outlines. However, no writing system could tolerate a state of affairs in which many words, especially very common words, took a long time to write. So, in another way, it is advantageous for words, especially common words, to be 'short' (have few letters). But it is more difficult for short words to be visually distinctive. So we have a trade-off situation which is resolved as follows:

1.   Some words are long. Their length gives them recognisability, therefore there is no reason why they should not be spelt phonically and in general *they are*, e.g. paradoxically, philanthropic, antidisestablishmentarianism.
2.   Some common words are very short. Here, the pressure for visual distinctiveness (combined with economy of symbol) far outweighs the pressure for phonic regularity and so these words are spelled 'graphically' and not phonically, e.g. of, do, so, was, were.

Even so, these words are also partly regular ('phonic'), in their spelling.

3.   The majority of words strike a balance between the two extremes. They are:
      fairly long/short and fairly regular/irregular.

All this explains why the shortest and commonest words of English are also the ones that are hardest to read off phonically. The consequences for teaching are well known:

> Short common words are hard to teach phonically but easy to teach by shape recognition ('look and say'). Longer, rarer, more interesting words are impossible to teach by 'look and say' but easy to teach phonically.

We can now proceed with our description of the English writing system.

The English Writing/Spelling System

Introduction

In our description we shall use the following general principles;

1. Not to concern ourselves too much with exceptions. A deviant spelling is either rare (by definition) or else covered by our remarks regarding the graphic spelling of common words. What is useful to the learner is *regularities*. So, for instance, there is little point in teaching <pt> as a spelling for /t/. A child who needs <ptarmigan> or <pterodactyl> will certainly finds ways of reading them.
2. We shall begin by looking at the *sounds* of English and considering how these are rendered by the *letters*. This is the linguistic approach. Then we shall put this information into reverse and consider how the letters of written language are pronounced or 'sounded' so as to reconstruct the spoken utterance. This is the teacher's approach. Both approaches have to be combined to arrive at an economical and useful description.
3. We shall confine ourselves at first to words of one syllable (monosyllables). The principles applying to words of more than one syllable (polysyllables) are different and will be considered separately.

Basic Facts About the English Writing System

Basic fact 1

Spoken English uses only a limited number of *contrastively different sounds*, which can be written down by means of a phonemic alphabet. Such an alphabet is provided in Appendix C and used throughout this book. Estimates of the total number of contrastive sounds used in a language will vary slightly according to the type of analysis being used – our figure is 44.

Basic fact 2

There are two kinds of *sound* in speech

- consonant *sounds* and
- vowel *sounds*.

(It is important not to confuse these with

- consonant *letters* and
- vowel *letters*,

which are dealt with below.)

Basic fact 3

Consonant sounds are made differently from vowel sounds. *Consonant sounds* are made by *blocking* or otherwise *constricting* the passage of air on its way out from the lungs.

> try /b/ – air is *trapped* behind closed lips, then released. (*blocking*)
> /s/ – air is *squeezed* out between the tip of the tongue and the roof of the mouth. (*constricting*)

Vowel sounds are made without blocking or constricting the outward flow of air. Instead, the resonating properties of the mouth are adjusted by shaping the lips and tongue and by raising and lowering the jaw.

> compare /i/ in key (/ki/) and
> /ɑ/ in car (/kɑ/).

Try saying /b/ and /s/ several times and then /i/ and /ɑ/ to get a feeling for the difference between consonant and vowel sound.

Basic fact 4

According to the usual analysis[6] there are 20 vowel *sounds* in English and 24 consonant *sounds*.
However   /r/ (*red*)
/j/ (*yellow*)
/w/ (*white*)

are *intermediate* as between consonant and vowel sound and so a more accurate summary would be

> 20 vowel sounds
> 3 intermediate sounds
> 21 consonant sounds

In other words, English uses approximately the same number of consonant *sounds* and vowel *sounds*.

Basic fact 5

English uses 26 *letters*, of which 21 are traditionally called *consonant letters* and 6 are traditionally called *vowel letters*. The discrepancy arises because <y> is considered (correctly) to be both a consonant letter and a vowel letter. In our analysis we shall treat

    <r> and
    <w>

as intermediate also–they are used both as consonant and as vowel letters.

While the traditional classification given above is largely accurate, it should be noted that consonant *letters* are sometimes used to help represent vowel *sounds*

    (e.g. /ʊ/ is spelt <oul> in *could*
    /ɔ/ is spelt <augh> in *caught*)

while

vowel letters sometimes help to contribute towards *consonant* sounds, (e.g. the letter <e> changes /hʌg/ (hug) to /hjudʒ/ (huge) and the letter <i> contributes to /ʃ/ in /p ɔʃn̩/ (portion).

Basic fact 6

There are just about enough consonant *letters* to go round, and in fact they are sometimes used one to one with corresponding consonant *sounds*.

e.g.   <p> ⟷ /p/ in <pitch>   /pɪtʃ/
          <t> ⟷ /t/ in <team>   /tim/

and so forth.

However, some consonant sounds are represented by *combinations*[7] of letters.

e.g.   /ð/ and /θ/ are represented by <th>–thy, thigh
       /tʃ/ by <(t)ch>–catch, peach
       /dʒ/ by <(d)ge>–badge, huge, region
       /ʃ/ by <sh, ti, ssi>–push, caution, passion
       /f/ (sometimes) by <gh ph>–enough, photo

We shall regard these combinations as composite letters which have to be learnt like the others.

Basic fact 7

There is a serious shortage of vowel letters. A ratio of 6 vowel *letters* to 20 vowel *sounds* means that anything like a 1:1 relation between vowel sounds and letters is impossible. The many shifts to which the written language resorts to make up for this shortage give rise to much overlapping and duplication and are a main reason for the complexity of the system.

The basic facts summarised

1. *Spoken English* employs only about 44 contrastively different *sounds*.
2. There are two kinds of spoken sound,
3.   *consonant* (airstream restricted) and
                     vowel (airstream flows freely)
4. /*spoken English*/ uses
                     20 vowel sounds
                     3 intermediate sounds
                     21 consonant sounds
5. <*written English*> uses
                     26 letters of which
                     21 are called consonant letters and
                     6 are called vowel letters
     <y>, being both vowel and consonant letter.
     In our treatment, <r> and <w> are also regarded as dual-purpose letters.
6. Although the alphabet contains a plentiful supply of consonant *letters*, it is still necessary to create additional consonant letters by grouping the basic letters into pairs (digraphs).
7. The shortage of vowel letters necessitates various contrivances including digraphs, trigraphs and 'silent e'.

The Shapes of the Letters

(We should remind ourselves at this point that the main object of a writing system is to provide distinctive and rapidly recognisable <words>. The system employs phonic means to achieve visual ends.)

The difference between vowel *letters* and consonant *letters* is striking. First, there is the difference in *number* which has already been noticed. Second, there is a difference of *shape*.

The vowel letters <a/ɑ e i o u> have hunched, rounded, rather neutral outlines as if their main function was to act as *spacers* for the consonant letters -nd -n f-ct -t -s n-t d-ff-c-lt t- r--d s-nt-c-s w-th n- --w-l l-tt-rs -n -t -ll -sp-cv-lly -f th-y h-v- pl-nty -f sp-ky c-nsn-nts. The -dd-tion -f j-st -ne v-wel letter m-k-es -ny -rd-n-ry text e-s-ly re-d-ble.

The consonant letters are much more imaginative in their use of the letter space. Eleven out of the 21 are ascenders or descenders

<b, d, f, g, h, j, k, l, p, q, t>

and <y> also proclaims its ambiguous status by its consonant type outline.[8]

The striking difference of shape between consonant letters and vowel letters seems to call for some explanation.

Perhaps one should remark first that the difference is necessary simply because there is a larger number of consonant letters and therefore a greater need to make them different from one another. But the 'spikiness' of consonant letters seems to be functional in another way as well – there is a kind of alliance between the visual distinctiveness of consonant letters and their phonic directness. If one accepts as a crude working generalisation the statement that spoken /words/ are composed of syllables and that a syllable tends to consist of a consonant sound (or sounds) followed by a vowel sound, as in the three syllables of

/bʌ - tə - flaɪ/

then we should expect to find, in longer words at any rate, a visual shape

– one could call it a c a s t e l l a t e d shape

which provides a sort of key to its syllabic structure.[9]

In other words, consonant letters make a crucial contribution to the message contained in a <word>, by relating in a direct way both to its sound pattern and to its outline.

The information thus conveyed is probabilistic rather than incremental but it is certainly employed both by fluent and by beginning readers as part of the process of probing guesswork which we mentioned on p. 135. A knowledge of the phonic values of the consonant letters (often conveyed by their names[10]) combined with a rough understanding of syllabic structure will evidently carry the beginning reader a long way into the task of decoding longer English <words>.

CONSONANT SOUNDS AND LETTERS. 'Is it true?' versus 'does it matter?'

In sketching the foundations for a phonic programme one is not aiming to give the pupil (or even necessarily the teacher) a complete account of the rules of the English writing system. Rather, the intention is to give the beginning reader just enough information to make a starting-point, or focus, or location, for supplementary information deriving from accumulating visual, syntactic and semantic cues. Phonic information is indispensable, but the less of it there is, the better. What we are setting out to purvey is *minimal* phonic information bearing in mind that dyslexics rely far more on phonic data than ordinary readers do.

Linguists and Teachers

To the linguist the written word (in alphabetic languages) is a form or rendering of the *spoken* word;

  /ketl̩/ *is rendered as* <kettle>

and so it is natural for linguistic writers to see written language in these terms.

In the example above

  /k/ is 'spelled' <k>
  /ɛ/ is 'spelled' <e>
  /t/ is 'spelled' <tt>
  /l̩/ is 'spelled' <le>

Teachers of reading, on the other hand, tend to approach the matter from the opposite standpoint – their pupils start from a printed or written text in which

  <k> 'says' /k/
  <e> 'says' /ɛ/
  <tt> 'says' /t/
  <le> 'says' /l̩/

Our treatment brings together both perspectives to produce an approach that is both linguistically sound and pedagogically appropriate. In the next section, we study the 'spelling' of the English consonant sounds. In later sections we discuss the 'saying' of the English consonant letters.

The Spelling of English Consonant Sounds

sound	how made	how spelled (regular)	e.g.	important variations	*name* of commonest letter + = useful* – = not useful
/b/	air trapped behind lips, then released	(b) b**	bubble		/biː/ +
/p/	air trapped behind lips, then released	(p) p	pepper		/piː/ +
/t/	air trapped behind tip of tongue, then released	(t) t	totter		/tiː/ +
/d/	air trapped behind tip of tongue, then released	(d) d	dodder		/diː/ +
/k/	air trapped behind back of tongue, then released	(c) k	kiss backer	(c) c (come accuse)	/keɪ/ + /siː/ –

* As a guide to pronunciation.
** (b)b means 'either <b> or double <b>' and so with other letters below.

sound	how made	how spelled (regular)	e.g.	important variations	*name* of commonest letter + = useful* − = not useful
/ʷ**k**/	as for /k/ but with rounded lips	qu	queen		/kju/ +
/g/	air trapped behind back of tongue, then released	(g) g	goggle	gh (ghost	/dʒi/ −
/ʃ/	air forced between tongue and roof of mouth	sh	push	ti (caution) ssi (mission)	
/ʒ/	air forced between tongue and roof of mouth	su si	pleasure explosion		/ɛs/ −
/tʃ/	air trapped behind tongue, then released slowly	(t) ch	rich hitch		(/eɪtʃ/)
/dʒ/	air trapped behind tongue then released slowly	j (d) g < i e	judge region large		/dʒeɪ/ + /dʒi/ −
/h/	air forced through throat	h	hit		/eɪtʃ/

* as a guide to pronunciation

Phoneme	Description	Spelling	Examples	Examples	Transcription	
/f/	air forced between lip and upper teeth	(f) f	from suffer	ph (photo) gh (rough)	/ɛf/	+
/v/	air forced between lip and upper teeth	v	over		/vi/	+
/θ/	air forced between tongue and upper teeth	th	bath		?	
/ð/	air forced between tongue and upper teeth	th	bathe		?	
/s/	air forced down groove in tongue	(s) s (t)	swim hiss bustle	ci city ce once cy fancy	/ɛs/ /si/	+ +
/z/	air forced down groove in tongue	(z) z	zoo, fuzz	si position so poison	/zɛd/ /zi/	+ +
/m/	air blocked by closed lips flows out through nose	(m) m	mammal		/ɛm/	+

sound	how made	how spelled (regular)	e.g	important variations	*name* of commonest letter + = useful* − = not useful	
/n/	air blocked by tongue flows out through nose	(n)	nunnery	kn knife	/ɛn/	+
/ŋ/	air blocked by back of tongue flows out through nose	nk ng nc	bank bang uncle		(/ɛn/)	?
/l/	air flows over side of tongue	(l) l	lolly		/ɛi/	+
/r/	air flows over tongue	(r) r	rage horror		/ɑ(r)/	?
/j/	tongue moves away from roof of mouth	y	young	i bullion	/waɪ/	−
/w/	lips open	w	west		/dʌblju/	−

Some comments on the 'Spelling' of English Consonant Sound and the 'Saying' of English Consonant Letters

The preceding account (which should form part of the professional equipment of all teachers of literacy) shows that the spelling of English consonant sounds is really quite straightforward; notice especially the small number of important variations and the general usefulness of letter *names* as a guide to their commonest associations.[11]

However, when one reverses the relationship and turns to the *sounding* or *pronunciation* of the consonant letters, certain problems emerge which have to be faced. Even so, it can be said that this set of relationships is relatively straightforward, too.

Some problems

1. Silent letters

When we start to reverse the rules, we find ourselves in a difficulty with the very first one.

<b/bb *is pronounced* ('says') /b (ə)/[12]

This is clear enough, but incomplete: there are also cases where <b> 'says' nothing at all as in *thumb* or *lamb*. The same phenomenon occurs with <l> in *palm* and <n> in *hymn*.

The best way to deal with this difficulty is to ignore it; the presence of <b> will not deter any child in practice from successfully reading *thumb*.

2. Digraphs

A much more serious problem arises with letter combinations (digraphs). It is true that

p	says	/p (ə)/
t	says	/t (ə)/
g	says	/g (ə)/
h	says	/h (ə)/
s	says	/s (ə)/
c	says	/k (ə)/

but what are these letters 'saying' when they appear in

    photo
    bath
    this
    rough
    shawl
    charm?

The spelling of /tʃ/, for instance, contains <c> and <h> but it obviously will not do to teach that these letters here have the values /k/ + /h/. The solution must be to treat <ch> as an additional composite letter with its own name and value /tʃ/. The idea of composite letters is, of course, a familiar one in the English writing system, <qu>, for instance, is a composite letter and the *double letters* are all 'composites' too. The use of the composite letters listed above allows more sounds to be represented and produces symbols that are even more shapely and distinct than those of single consonant letters.

3. Divergence, convergence, overlap

<g> and <j> show these problems in a simple form:

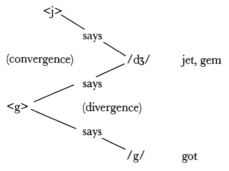

<c> and <s> give a more complex patten

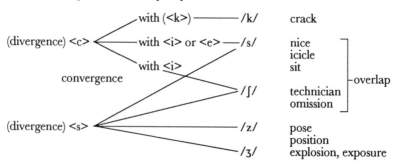

The Saying of English Consonant Letters

letter shape	letter name	sound	examples
1. Straightforward			
<b/bb>	/bi/	/b(ə)/	blubber
<p/pp>	/pi/	/p(ə)/	pepper
<f/ff>	/ɛf/	/f/	from, suffer
<v/(vv)>	/vi/	/v/	vine, hover (bovver)
<z/zz>	/zɛd/,/zi/	/z/	zoo, fuzz
<d/dd>	/di/	/d(ə)/	debt, sudden
<m/mm>	/ɛm/	/m/	mammal
<n/nn>	/ɛn/	/n/	ninny
<kn>	/keɪɛn/	/n/	knife
<ng>	/ɛndʒi/	/ŋ/	bang, singer
<l/ll>	/ɛl/	/l/	lull, lolly
<w(h)>	/dʌbljʊ/	/w/	west, when

[See also <w> as a VOWEL letter]

letter shape	letter name	sound	examples	
2. The <h> group				
<h>	/eɪtʃ/	/h/	how	
<sh>	/ʃ(ə)/	/ʃ/	shelf	
<th>	/θ(ə)/	/θ/	thistle	It can be noted
<th>	/ð(ə)/	/ð/	this, bother	that each of
<ch>	/tʃ(ə)/	/tʃ/	chest	these has <h>
<ph>	/f(ə)/	/f/	photo	as a second letter
<gh>	/dʒieɪtʃ/	/f/[13]	rough	

letter shape	letter name	sound	examples
3. <j> and <g>			
<j>	/dʒeɪ/	/dʒ/	just (always pronounced /dʒ/)
<g>	/dʒi/	/dʒ/	gin, gem (only when followed by <i> or <e>)
		/g(ə)/	grim, gold, guilty (only when *not* followed by <i> or <e>)

letter shape	letter name	sound	examples
4. <s>, <c> and <k>			
<s/ss/sc>	/ɛs/	/s/	sissy, scientific
		/ʃ/	mission, conscience
		/z/	cause
		/ʒ/	explosion

<c/cc/ck>	/si/	/s/	city, once, access, fancy (/s/ when followed by <i> <e> or <y>)
	/k/		cracker, occur (/k/ otherwise)
<k>	/keɪ/	/k/	kill

5. <t> and <ti>

| <t/tt> | /ti/ | /t(ə)/ | team, tattoo |
| <ti> | /tiaɪ/ | /ʃ/ | initiation |

6. <r>

| <r/rr> | /a(r)/ | /r/ | run, warren |
| | | or /∅/ (zero) | farm |

Note. The letter <r> often occurs in situations where it will be pronounced or left silent depending on the *variety* of English being used. For instance, in Australian English and in 'Northern' British English, the <r> is silent in *car* and *farm*, but it is pronounced in, for instance, Scots and American English. Teaching should take this into account.

7. <x>, <y>, <qu>

<x>	/ɛks/	/ks/	box
		/gz/	exit
<y>	/waɪ/	/j/	yield (<y> is also a *vowel* letter and will be further discussed under that heading)
<qu>	/kju/	/ʷk/	queen (<q> forms a composite letter with <u>)

A Note on Consonant Clusters

Languages differ in the consonant *sounds* that they permit at the beginnings and endings of syllables. For instance, English syllables do *not* begin with /nk/, /mr/, or /ŋ/ (last sound in *sing*) but these initial combinations are permitted in some languages.

/nk/ occurs initially in some African languages (<Nkomo>)
/mr/ occurs initially in Serbo-Croat (surname <Mroczek>)
/ŋ/ occurs initially in Maori (first name <Ngaio>)

These rules and restrictions will of course be reflected in the spelling systems of the languages concerned.

/ps/ occurred in Classical Greek and has been retained in the *spelling* of several words brought into English from that language (*pseudo, psychology, psalm*), but it has been 'anglicised' to /s/ in the pronunciation.

Because these sound combinations (known technically as *clusters*) often give rise to spelling problems, we have taken this opportunity to display below most of the clusterings that are permitted at the beginnings and endings of English syllables. It is important to remember that these all relate to consonant *sounds*. Readers may find it interesting and valuable to discover a word that exemplifies each *sound* combination. A few examples are supplied in brackets. We begin with pairs of consonant sounds that are allowed at the beginnings of English syllables.[14]

Initial Clusters of Two Consonant Sounds

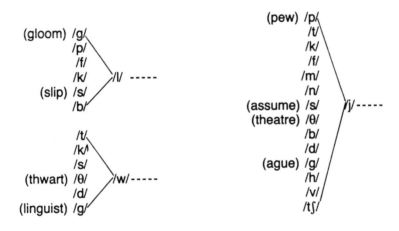

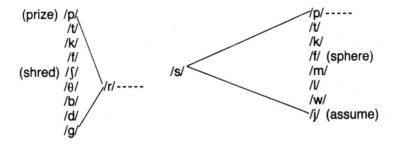

Initial Clusters of Three Consonant Sounds

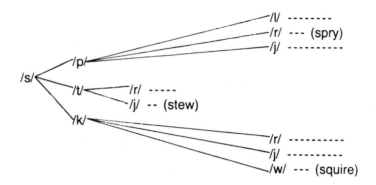

Final Clusters of Two Consonant Sounds

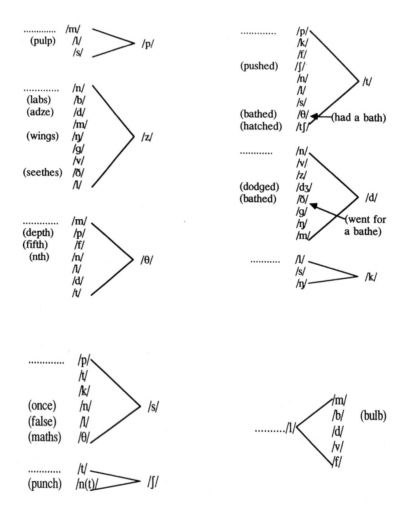

There are a few *three-member final clusters*

    e.g. /lfθ/ (<twelfth>)

and even one or two *four-member final clusters*

    e.g. /mpst/ (<glimpsed>).

Notes for Teachers

Our treatment of the consonant sounds and letters of English suggests some ideas which might be helpful to teachers.

1. Work on the sounds

English uses a limited number of well-defined consonant sounds which are represented by a perfectly manageable number of clearly distinguishable visual patterns (29 in our analysis). *This is a very helpful pedagogical feature.* Children should be given plenty of practice in making the sounds and in associating them with the corresponding shapes. They should be given some information accompanied by practical work on how the consonant sounds are made (the second column on p. 150–3). They should also be made thoroughly familiar with the idea that */words/ are analysable into sounds* by being invited

a.   to produce and imitate sounds,
b.   to supply words that begin and end with certain sounds ('Tell me a word that begins with /f/ and ends with /z/') (fizz)
c.   to produce rhymes for given words ('What rhymes with fizz? What sound does that begin and end with? '... and so on.)

Vowel sounds can be glossed over at this stage – an indispensable art for the beginning reader.
    In summary; *reading lessons should contain plenty of oral work on sounds.*

2. Phonics is an aid to reading and not an end in itself

As far as possible, words should be read in context and not in isolation. Hold-ups should not be allowed to build to frustration point, but instead the reader should be encouraged either to go back and redevelop what has gone before or to push on to build up some more context, or both. The student should have the *sensation* that all contextual clues are being brought to bear.

3. The pupil should be accustomed to the idea of irregularities and exceptions in phonic structure

For instance, there are exceptions to the rules given on p. 155.

> <g> is /g/ before <e> in <get> (should be /dʒ/)
> <f> is /v/ in <of>

and so forth, but these variations are unimportant because the beginning reader will not be troubled by them unless the teacher is.

In the same way (but with some misgivings), we have omitted the correspondence between <*ch*> and /*k*/ from our treatment because this spelling occurs mainly in more advanced words like *chaos, chorus, character* and *chrysanthemum*, which are infrequent in the earlier stages of reading. When they do crop up, the reader will be ready to take them in his or her stride (with the help of contextual clues.)

The overall aim should be a minimum phonics which is taught in an undogmatic way and which addresses itself to that great bulk of words that are intermediate both in frequency and in regularity.

4. The sounding of consonants

It has become a touchstone of enlightenment *not* to sound schwa (/ə/) after consonant sounds spoken in isolation and no doubt the element of self-deception inherent in this article of faith is very harmless. Nonetheless, it is a fact that even a phonetician would find it difficult to pronounce isolated plosive sounds like /b/, /t/ without a following vocalic sound. An intolerable conflict between politeness and scientific rigour has been resolved by inserting schwa (in brackets) after plosive articulations and omitting it after continuant articulations (/m/, /v/) which are easy to say by themselves.

Sticking sounds together to form words does give rise to problems, and pupils should be given plenty of practice in 'slurring', for instance /k(ə)-æ-t(ə)/ into /kæt/

5. It sometimes turns out on enquiry that children have rather strange ideas about what reading actually is. So it should be explained that they are trying by all means to find out 'what it says' (to use the conventional and perfectly acceptable phrase); it should also be explained that word shapes can be helpful (flash cards can be used to make this point) and that guessing is all right too, as long as it is sensible.

We mean this advice to be taken quite literally: there should be occasional planned moments of discussion introduced by questions

('What are you trying to do when you read?') which are pursued in a systematic way.

English Vowel Sounds and Letters; A Minimum Treatment

Dialectal variation

The speech sounds which a child first brings to school will have been formed by association with immediate family and friends and may not be the ones that the teacher regards as correct or suitable for use in explaining letter–sound correspondences. To such children, the first reading lesson will come as a severe culture shock from which some, at least, will not recover. We have already drawn attention to the correlation between late reading and socio-economic stratum; it can hardly be a coincidence that the social group with the widest range of dialectal variation[15] is also the group with the highest incidence of reading difficulty. Even teachers who are unprejudiced in this respect may still lack the skill to translate their ideas into teaching practice. The problem can be, and probably has been, sidetracked to a certain extent by avoiding phonic methods, but this means abandoning the direct route to success in early reading not only for dyslexics but for ordinary readers too. One handicap is merely replaced by another. In any case the underlying dissonance remains.

The correct solution, bearing in mind that dialectal variation is largely concentrated in *vowel sounds,* is

1.   To accept that people in different parts of the English speaking world use *widely* differing letter/vowel sound correspondences,
2.   To recognise that *the writing system is not tied to any particular standard or variety of speech.*
3.   To ascertain what system your pupils use.
4.   To make use of it in your teaching.

The description of vowel sounds and vowel letters which follows is necessarily based on a single pronunciation – the one normally taught to foreigners – but it is important that it should be modified and adapted to suit local conditions.

English Vowel Sounds, A Classification

English vowel sounds are generally divided into *short* and *long:* an idea which is of rather doubtful phonetic validity[16] but which does reflect the way that sounds are treated in the English writing system. For that reason we are adopting it here.

Short vowel sounds

Short vowel *sounds* are sounds that can be *represented* in words of one syllable by a single vowel letter, followed by a single consonant letter. The range of 'short' vowel sounds ('Southern') is

/æ/ (bag) /ɛ/ (beg) /ɪ/ (big) /ɒ/ (bog) /ʌ/ (bug)
but some dialects omit /æ/ and substitute /ʌ/, giving the range ('Northern')
/ʌ/ /bʌg/ (bag), /ʊ/ /bʊg/ (bug), /ɛ/ /bɛg/ (beg), /ɪ/ /bɪg/ (big), /ɒ/ /bɒg/ (bog).

The 'Northern' pronunciation for the letter <u> is used by Southerners in *put* /pʊt/.

In the definition above, '*can* be represented' does not mean '*must* be represented'; so for instance the vowel letters in *bank, bend, list, font, bust, push,* all have 'short' values but are followed by *two* consonant letters.

Long vowel sounds

We shall define long vowel sounds as those vowel sounds which *cannot be represented* in monosyllables by a single vowel letter followed only by a single consonant letter. So, for instance, /aɪ/ is long in *bite,* (needs <e> as well as the consonant letter), and in *wild* (needs two consonant letters).

We shall say that <y>, <r> and <w> are dual-purpose letters – vowel letters as well as consonant letters – so *pay, car* and *saw* will not be exceptions to this definition – /eɪ/, /ɑ/ and /ɔ/ are 'long' sounds.

A list of the spellings of English long vowel sounds is given below. In broad terms they are spelled either with *silent e* (*cake*) or with *digraphs* (*freak*) or with following consonant clusters or combinations (*cold, branch*), or by a single vowel letter with no following letters (fly). Combinations of these methods are possible (*beach*).

Schwa (ə)

Schwa is neither long nor short in our definition, since it does not occur in (stressed) monosyllables at all, at least not in the dialect that we have adopted for our description. It is, however, very common in polysyllables and we shall discuss it briefly here for the sake of completeness.

It is a fact of English that vowel sounds that are weakened in *stress* sometimes change their *pronunciation* as well. (A full discussion of stress is given elsewhere in Book Three.) In such cases, the 'new' pronunciation is often schwa.

In the table below, a syllable is first shown in *stressed* position. Then the same syllable is shown in *unstressed* position as part of a longer word. In each case, the vowel becomes schwa (/ə/).

Stressed Syllables (various vowel sounds)			Same syllable unstressed (becomes schwa)	
pot	(/pɒt/) becomes /pət/	in)	potato	(/pəteɪtəʊ/)
ward	(/wɔd/) becomes /wəd/	in)	awkward	(ɔkwəd/)
path	(/pɑθ/) becomes /pəθ/	in)	sympathy	(sɪmpəθɪ/)
tent	(/tɛnt/) becomes /tant/	in)	inconsistent	(/ɪnkənsɪstent/)

In the next sections we treat the English vowel letters and sounds in much the same way that we treated the English consonant letters and sounds. That is to say we first set down a complete list of vowel *sounds* and consider how they are *spelled* (linguist's approach); then we reverse these rules in order to arrive at a *pronunciation* of the English vowel *letters* (teacher's approach). Once again, both approaches are necessary in order to produce an economical and teachable description. The sound/letter correspondences for vowels are not as tidy and straightforward as the ones for consonants but still they are not too bad.

Our analysis produces 28 consonant letters and letter groups and about 20 vowel letters and letter groups (depending on how one reckons it).

The Spelling of English Vowel Sounds in Monosyllables

Short vowel sounds

Short sounds	Favourite letter	Spelling, e.g.
/æ/	a	bag, had, badge, pant
/ɛ/	e	beg, fed, ledge, sent
/ɪ/	i	big, hid, list, lilt
/ɒ/	o	bog, lot, pond, (*but* salt, wasp, want)
/ʌ/	u	bug, but, butt, bung, (replaced by /ʊ/ in some varieties)

Notes

[1]   More properly, they represent an abstraction from the sounds of spoken language–see 'Phoneme and graphemes', p. 140.

[2]   It is somewhat misleading to distinguish between the perception of words alternatively as 'sequences of letters' or as 'distinct visual shapes' (e.g. Goswami and Bryant, 1990, Chapter 2), since a sequence of letters is also a distinct visual shape. See Bertelson's reference (1986, p.9) to 'the direct orthographic reading of the skilled adult, where typically all the available orthographic evidence is taken account of...a small change in a single interior letter of a word highly predictable from context still disrupts reading performance...'

[3]   Contextualisation. Some readers have found this term rather forbidding. It means simply the skill of guessing words through the combined meanings of adjacent words. The reading of the example sentence is helped by knowing that people shoot at, and sometimes miss, targets. More about contextualisation on p. 179.

[4]   See N. Ellis (Snowling and Thomson, 1991, Chapter 6) for a 'rise and fall' survey of teaching methods from early times and a reasoned defence of phonic approaches: ' ...we do believe that it is advisable for beginning readers and those who are backward or specifically handicapped to be assisted in developing facility in dissecting a word's sound structure so as to foster symbol–sound and sound–symbol association. At times this must involve the direct teaching of these associations.'

[5]   Stuart and Coltheart (1988) have produced evidence to suggest that children make use of phonological skills (in conjunction with letter–sound knowledge) from the earliest stages of the reading process and that the level of phonological skills in a nursery-class child is a good predictor of eventual progress.

[6]   E.g. Wells and Colson (1974). Our own analysis is slightly different but the total is the same.

[7]   Sometimes called **digraphs** — two letters representing a single sound or **trigraphs** — three letters representing a single sound. Quadragraphs exist as well.

[8]   Of the less spiky remainder, it could be said that <r, w, m, n> all relate to sounds that partake somewhat of the vocalic.

9   Of course 'descending' consonants provide visual clues below the line as well as above it.

10 Letter names. Without wishing to labour the point, it can be stated that 14 out of the 21 consonant letter names are directly helpful in suggesting their spoken counterparts, while c, q, g, r, y are of some assistance. Only h and w are quite unhelpful and even <h> (/eitʃ/) has some relation to the common use of <h> in forming digraphs <ch>, <sh>. (All the vowel letter names are directly helpful.)

11 This assertion can be checked very easily by seeing whether the sound in the left-hand column recurs in the right-hand column.

12 See 'The sounding of consonants', on p. 161.

13 Other terminal occurrences of <gh> (through, bough) are silent.

14 For a good general discussion of syllable structure, see Barbara Strang, Modern English Structure, 1962, from which these data have been extracted.

15 See M. Trudgill, Sociolinguistics, 1974, pp. 41–42.

16 For instance, in terms of actual duration the 'short' /æ/ in bad will be 'as long as any of the long vowels' Gimson 1962, Compare the 'long' /i/ in beet, beef.

17 /ʊ/ is 'long' in South, 'short' in North.

Long vowel sounds

Long sounds	Favourite letter(s)	Single V letter + no C letter	Groups of V letters + no C letter	Single V letter + C letter + silent <e>	Single V letter + group of C letters	Group of V letter + C letter(s)
				Spellings e.g.		
/eɪ/	a ⟨i / y⟩	a (accented)	pay, say	pane, gate	(strange)	straight, rain, rein, weigh
/i/	e	he, she; we, me	free, flea	scene, cede, scheme		mean, fiend, siege, feet
/aɪ/	i, y	I, why; sky; fly	guy, buy	mine, pride, style, while	might, pint, mind, isle, wild, high, sight	

/əʊ/	o	go so no	owe, bow toe sew slow	lone note	don't won't most post	load own though boast
/u/ /ju/	u ou oo	do (to)	too woo crew, stew you due	tune rude move		groove moon through juice youth
/ʊ/ [17]	(o)u	to			full, pull push	would, book look, good
/ɑ/	a(r)	ma	far car are		half past, raft palm chance staff, path plant	farm laugh park (much regional variation)

Long sounds	Favourite letter(s)	Spellings, e.g.				
		Single V letter + no C letter	Groups of V letters + no C letter	Single V letter + C letter + silent \<e\>	Single V letter + group of C letters	Group of V letter + C letter(s)
/ɔ/	o?		door poor paw gnaw store or, oar awe, ore more drawer		call all tall talk stalk	ought caught court fought taught born cord
/ɜ/	e(r)? r?		err her were purr stir fur	(\<r\> is sounded in some varieties)		nerve earn swerve burn burst shirt dirt hurt bird

/aʊ/	o $\langle$ w, u	how, now bow	brown, out loud, crowd
/ɔɪ/	o $\langle$ i, y	boy, joy	join, hoist
/ɪə/	e...r	ear, pier sneer, fear	beard weird
/ɛə/	r?	air pair prayer pear there dare	bairn laird (Scotish)

Neither long nor short

/ə/	none	Only occurs in unstressed monosyllables (e.g. *but*, *of*) and in polysyllables. (regional variation)

The 'sayings' of English Vowel Letters in Monosyllables

Letter or letter group	Pronounciation, e.g.				
	'short'	'silent e'	terminal	consonant + letters	other spellings of same sound
The <a> group					
<a/ɑ>	/æ/ **bank** **lag**	/eɪ/ **gate**			
ai ˄ ˅ ay		/eɪ/	pay tray	gain straight faint fail paint	rein weigh vein
<ar>		/ɑ/	far car star scar jar	farm cart part harm	palm, calm, half past, chance, path staff, laugh (much regional variation in pronounciation)

Grapheme	Pronunciation	Examples		Irregular
<air> air > are <	/ɛə/	air stair lair fair fare stare care	(bairn)	prayer pear, there heir their mayor

The <e> group

Grapheme	Pronunciation	Examples	Pronunciation	Examples		Irregular
<e>	/ɛ/	beg egg	/i/	scene scheme me be		
<ee> <ea>			/i/	fee free flea pea	mean, please lean, dream steel fleet	fiend seige
er ir > ur <			/ɜ/	her, err fur, fir stir purr, were	nerve swerve, jerk burn, burst dirt, shirt first, hurt bird, germ	earn learn

Letter or letter group	Pronunciation, e.g				
	'short'	'silent e'	terminal	consonant letters +	other spellings of same sound
The \<i\> group					
\<i/y\>	/ɪ/ bit hill list print	/aɪ/ pride style while bite white fire spire	/aɪ/ I, by buy, pry why, pie sky, guy my, try		
\<igh\>		/aɪ/	high sigh	might fright	night sight
			↑		
The \<o\> group					
\<o\>	/ɒ/ cot, pond pot, pod odd	/əʊ/ ode note	/əʊ/ go no	both don't won't ghost most	(/ɒ/) was, wasp, want salt, fault

oa > /əʊ/ ow <	low, tow sow, grow slow	loaf road groan own coast boast	though yolk dough folk
ow > /aʊ/ ou <	how, now bow, sow row, brow our, hour	out, frown shout, stout crowd, round howl	plough
or > aw /ɔ/ augh <	(for) or, ore bore, store gnaw, saw store, floor awe, claw	port caught fort born	ought, court all, call, fall drawer, oar, fought tall, talk, stalk
oi > /ɔɪ/ oy <	boy toy joy ploy	join coin soil toil hoist	

Letter or letter group	Pronunciation, e.g				
	'short'	'silent e'	terminal	consonant + letters	other spellings of same sound
The \<u\> group **\<u\>**	**/ʌ/** **bug** **bust** **hunt**	**/(j)u/** **tune, rude** **duke, dude** **cute, rule**	**/(j)u/** due		
\<ew, oo, ui, ui\>		/(j)u/ ⟶	pew, too crew, you woo, stew	groove moon juice cruise youth boot, newt suit food	do through
\<u/oo\>		/ʊ/ ⟶	to (unstressed)	foot book put, full wood push look good bull	would, could

Chapter 2
The English writing system: polysyllables and longer sequences

Introduction

The rules for the reading and spelling of *monosyllables,* which have been described in the preceding sections, are rules which must be 'known' by every reader whether he or she has actually been taught them or not, but knowing them is only the first stage on the way to fluent reading. Ordinary readers, probably, and dyslexic readers, certainly, need teachers who are able to understand and teach the processes which come into play as the reader begins to approach more difficult texts[1] or, for that matter, when he or she wants to read easy texts with maximum speed and minimum effort.

Polysyllables

As texts become more difficult, the reader can expect to encounter a widening range of longer words (polysyllables) which demand a correspondingly wider range of reading skills. These will not necessarily be skills which the reader already has and which need merely to be strengthened and reinforced; on the contrary, some of the techniques and understandings that are now required will be different from, and even in contradiction to, the ones that went along with the initial reading of monosyllables.

At the phonic level, for instance, it is evident that *<rope>* in *rope* (/rəʊp/) is a much different proposition from *<rope>* in

Europe (/jɜː/ˌ rəp/) or in *European* (/jɜː/ˌ rəpiən/)

similarly with <app> in *apple, apply* and with <cat> in *cat, catastrophe.*

We shall discuss this feature further when we come to deal with *syllable* and *stress.*

Interactivity

An extremely important but much less obvious development which also goes along with the enlargement of reading skills is that words, whether long or short, begin to generate new relationships among themselves and to draw the reader more and more into an interactive process whereby words function together as part of a sequence which, in turn, is embedded in a text, so that each word is somehow able to illuminate, and to be illuminated by, the words that surround it. This interchange (which occurs to an extent within words as well as between them) evidently calls on new skills of prediction and contextualisation on the part of the reader. Before going on to develop these ideas it will be helpful to remind ourselves of some points that were made at the beginning of Book Three. A slightly modified version of the relevant sections follows below.

Basics of the Reading Process (Revisited)

Scanning the lines

Reading is the act of decoding written or printed <words> so as to arrive at their meaning. Fluent reading is the act of decoding written or printed words so as to arrive at the meaning of a *text*.

The writing system takes great care to make words visually distinct and easily recognisable: every word is separated from adjacent words by spaces, and every word is given its own special 'spelling' which never changes.

However, fluent readers do not 'sound out' or otherwise analyse a text word by word. Instead, they scan the lines in a rapid and complex way which allows them at any given moment to be

interpreting the current text reviewing what has gone before building up an impression of what is to come (Figure 17).

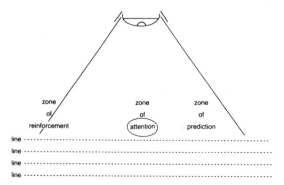

Figure 17. Optics of the reading process.

Sifting the information

Linked to, and interwoven with, the complex visual process of optical scanning there is an equally complex mental process, best described as 'probing guess work', which gathers, sifts and co-ordinates the four different kinds of information carried by <*words*>, namely,

> phonic information
> graphic information
> semantic information
> syntactic information

Beginning readers operate the same processes of scanning and sifting as fluent readers do but far less efficiently. Their reading improves as their guesswork improves.

The writing system is designed for fast reading and is functional for that purpose.

The Linguistics of the Reading Process

Written words carry four kinds of information which are 'read off' simultaneously in the decoding process:

1. *Phonic information*
   Written <words> represent the *sounds* (see Chapter 1, note **1**) of corresponding spoken /words/ (<sit> represents /sit/). This aids *reconstruction*.
2. *Graphic information*
   Words have characteristic and individual *designs*. (<ruff>, has a different shape from <rough>(see Chapter 1, note **2**)). This aids *recognition*.
3. *Semantic information*
   Words have *meaning*. ('The shot missed the t--g-t'). This aids *contextualisation*.(see Chapter 1, note **3**).
4. *Syntactic information*
   Words have *grammatical potential*.
   (' a ---- of -----.' *permits* 'a want of sense' but *precludes* 'a went of since'). This aids *prediction*.

The teaching of reading has been dominated by schools of thought which have each tended to emphasise the importance of one kind of information while devaluing the others. In fact all four modes

phonic
graphic
semantic
syntactic

are of equal importance for fluent reading.

Having dealt quite fully in the preceding sections with *phonic* and *graphic* aspects of a written text, we now proceed to examine *semantic* and *syntactic* aspects and the relationship between *all four* modes.

More about the reading process. The written language as a 'signal'.

In the preceding sections we have been concerned mainly with the *phonic* and *graphic* components of the written signal and with the mental processes which correspond to these components and which we have called *reconstruction* and *recognition*. These two processes go on simultaneously and help each other. We bring to them our knowledge of the shapes and sounds of the letters and of the 'rules' of spelling.

We now consider the last two kinds of information, *semantic* and *syntactic*, and the mental processes which correspond to them and which we have called *contextualisation* and *prediction*.

These two processes go on simultaneously and help each other. We bring to them our knowledge of the *world* and our knowledge of *language*.

The simultaneous interaction of *all four processes* is what makes it possible for us to read 'fluently' – that is, at a rate which keeps pace with the speed of mental activity. (Figure 18).

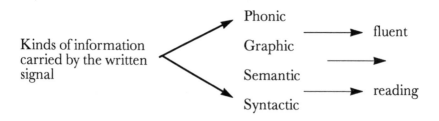

Figure 18. Fluent reading.

Semantic Information; Contextualisation; Attention

It is perhaps rather obvious that the fluent reader does not give equal attention to every single word in a text. For instance a reading of the sentence

'In England you don't need a licence for a dog or even for a ---.'

builds up very strong expectations about the word that is likely to occur in the final slot and the letters that actually do occupy that space will be attended to only to the extent that they fulfil or defeat those presuppositions. Clues that confirm *cat* will convey very little information that is unexpected or 'new' and will receive correspondingly little attention from the reader – much less than would be required to read *cat* in the ordinary or classroom sense of that word. The 'inner reader' is therefore, and to that extent, set free to move on to the exploration of new meanings.

The ability to contextualise like this evidently adds up to a very important saving of time and effort, especially when it is spread over an entire text. This particular instance depended on the reader's knowledge of England as a country where dogs and cats are the commonest pets, frequently thought of together but regarded differently in the eyes of the law. A foreigner who lacks this knowledge must read the text more closely at this point and so must we if anything happens to disturb our expectation of *cat*. If, for instance, the first 'scan' suggested that the word in question was not phono/graphically reconcilable with *cat,* then a closer reading would be needed to establish *jellyfish* or *grandmother.* Or the reader's awareness of the writer as a satirical fellow with an interest in wildlife preservation might put him or her on guard for *bat* or *cod.* We can define contextualisation at this point as the process whereby a reader brings to bear his or her knowledge of life in general and of the particular setting within which a writer is operating so as to *reduce uncertainty* about the content of a written/printed text. Without such advance knowledge of 'what a writer is talking about' reading becomes a much more laborious activity, as we soon discover when we come to deal with closely argued texts on unfamiliar topics.

Syntactic Features: Preliminary Discussion

Even so, and even in the absence of semantic information, the possibilities for the final slot of the sentence in the example above will still be significantly restricted by what we shall be calling 'syntactic' features which here, as always, interact with 'semantic' features, so as to reduce the potential load on the reader's attention. In this particular instance we 'know' that a single item following *a* must be a *noun*. Even if the reader has no idea what a noun is, he or she still knows very well that *chair* is possible in such a situation, and that *why*, *yet*, or *marginally* is not. Still another kind of knowledge tells the reader that a word following *a* has to begin with a consonant *sound*: *university* is possible but not *umbrella*. We could summarise this part of the discussion by saying that *a* in this, or any context has zero semantic force but major syntactic force.

Before going on to discuss syntactic features in detail we should say something more about the important features of written language which allow a fluent reader to narrow the focus of attention and to proceed on an accumulating balance of probabilities. Our comments on this central and crucial process will be gathered under the general heading of *redundancy*.

Redundancy

What is redundancy?

Figure 18, reproduced below, indicated a relationship between the four modes which combine interactively to produce the written 'message' or 'signal'.

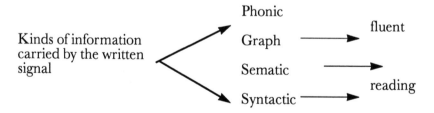

Figure 18. Fluent reading.

This diagram also suggests that our ability to *receive* and *interpret* the four modes simultaneously is what accounts for fluent reading (reading which keeps up with the speed of mental events).

One way of expressing this idea would be to say that the written signal is carried on four channels (phonic, graphic, semantic, syntactic) and this would be true up to a point. However, it is not the case that the four channels add up to the message carried by the signal, with each channel contributing about 25%, but rather it is the case that each channel contains the whole message, or almost the *whole message*, so that a reader is, at any given moment, receiving the 'same' message four times over. Since it should theoretically be enough to get the message *once*, we can say that three-quarters of the information we receive as readers is *superfluous* or *redundant*.

For a much simplified analogy we can consider the case of a general who wishes a dispatch to be carried across hostile territory and who entrusts four copies (of the same message) to four different messengers.

The *redundancy* of his signal is achieved by a somewhat extravagant use of manpower, but it makes excellent sense in a military context because it increases by a factor of four the likelihood that his message will 'get through' to the person for whom it is intended.

In fact, the written signal contains far more redundancy than we have made appear since each 'channel' not only contributes to the four-fold ('parallel') redundancy of the written message, but also carries its own 'built-in' ('serial') redundancy. We shall illustrate this point by reference only to the *graphic* channel.

'Built-in' Redundancy of the Graphic Channel

1. *Vowel letters* are largely redundant.
    It is commonplace to remark th-t wr-tt-n l-ng--g- is l-rg-ly c-mpr-h-ns-bl- w-th--t v-w-l l-tt-rs.

    However, since we do use vowel letters, it follows that more information than necessary is being transmitted on the graphic channel.

2. *All* letters, are largely redundant.
    This can easily be demonstrated by covering a line of writing or print with a piece of card and slowly sliding it down until the text becomes readable,

    A half exposure will be more than sufficient

    much the same thing happens

    when the print is uncovered from the bottom edge.
    We print whole lines of print when half lines would do.

3. *Abbreviations*
    Most people who take notes have tried to save time by making extensive use of abbreviations. This is effective up to a certain point, but the advantage tends to be nullified by the need to write more slowly and distinctly in order to preserve compre-

hensibility. One could say that one kind of graphic redundancy (the spelling system) is here being traded off against another (the redundancy of letter shapes). More accurate shapes are needed to compensate for the loss of full spelling. If one has terrible handwriting the net gain may be quite small.

4.   Where *precision* is particularly important it may be necessary to increase still further the redundancy of the written signal on the twin messenger principle described above. This occurs when letters and figures are both used to specify the sum of money to be transferred by a cheque.

Why is redundancy?

We shall distinguish three ways in which redundancy promotes the effectiveness of the written message by providing

1.   Robustness
2.   Speed
3.   Informativeness

1. *Robustness* will be the quality which enables the message to 'get through' in spite of 'noise'. Noise will be whatever might tend to interfere with the reception of the message.

For example
(in spoken language)
        in hostile territory ....enemy scouts

on radio	atmospherics
on television	interference
at a political meeting	heckling
at a party	surrounding chatter

(in written language)

in reading	bad light
	small print
	illegible handwriting

A signal that is highly repetitive and/or particularly rich in information is likely to do best under these conditions. For instance, the exuberance of our spelling system helps words to survive the degraded signal resulting from unclear handwriting. This is one respect among several in which the English spelling system turns out to be functional.

2. *Speed*

Because the message is carried simultaneously in four modes ('channels'), each of which contains additional built-in redundancy, the signal is extremely rich in information and can therefore be coded in a highly compressed form. Figure 19 expresses this idea diagramatically.

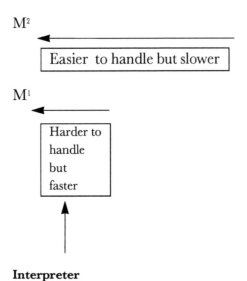

M²

Easier to handle but slower

M¹

Harder to
handle
but
faster

Interpreter

Figure 19. 'Richness' helps speed. The less concentrated message (M²) takes longer to get past the interpreting point than the more concentrated M¹.

M is the *Message* reaching the *interpreter* in two modes M^1 and M^2, which both have the same content (area). M^2 is less compressed than M^1 (more spread out) and will be easier to process than M^1 (because less needs to be done at any given moment) but it will take longer to pass the *interpreter*. M^1 is correspondingly harder to process than M^2 (more is happening at any given moment), but it will pass the interpreter more quickly.

All this is, of course, dependent on the Interpreter being equipped for the rapid processing of complex information. This condition is fulfilled in the case of written language which is perfectly adapted for fast processing by the human brain for the excellent reason that it was designed by the human brain in the first place. Written, no less than spoken language, is an embodiment of human mental function.

3. *Informativeness*

This is the property of written language which allows different aspects of the signal to cross-refer to each other and sustain each other so that greater certainty on one channel can compensate at any point for less certainty on another. One could say that the four channels are able to 'talk to' (*inform*) each other. *Informativeness* is one of the most striking features of the written signal and also one of the least discussed, no doubt because it is difficult to present such an elusive phenomenon in a simple way, or at all. The following *examples* give a necessarily crude and incomplete impression of an infinitely complex and finely tuned process.

a. The semantic channel can 'inform' the others.
In the sentence

'Would you draw the curtains please?'

the word *draw* is uncertain ('ambiguous') at the phonic, graphic and syntactic levels (is it *open/close* or *make a sketch of?*); the sounds, the letters and the grammatical functions would do equally well for either interpretation, but at the semantic/contextual level (proximity of *curtains*) uncertainty is reduced almost to zero. This kind of clear-cut situation (*either/or*) is relatively uncommon. The next examples illustrate the more usual situation in which clues from several channels are combining to nudge the reader towards a correct interpretation of the text.

b. The *graphic* mode can 'inform' the others.
(i) Help with contextualisation.
Several writers have observed that English has not one spelling system but rather two or three subsystems or styles of spelling which correspond in a general way to the *source language* of the word in question. (See Albrow, K.H. The English Writing System, (1972.) Thus, words which come directly from a Graeco/Roman source (*pentathlon*) or from Anglo-Saxon (*thoroughbred*) will have a rather distinctive graphical flavour, while 'Romance' words (Graeco-Roman filtered through Norman French) will occupy a position somewhere in between (*defence*).

Since the Anglo/Saxon part of our vocabulary has a well known if somewhat overestimated tendency to refer to the earthier side of life, while Graeco/Latin vocabulary inclines towards the more rarefied and scientific, it follows that a spelling system which draws on several sources will have the capacity to throw out a steady stream of small hints about the contextual flavour of the subject matter under discussion. By way of illustration we could consider a list of spellings for the sound /saɪ/ at the beginning of words. For example,

<sigh-> \
<psi-> \
<si-> \
<sci-> \
<sig-> \
<ci-> \
<cy-> \
<psy->

The reader is invited now, and before reading the footnote, to write down one or more words beginning with each group of letters, and then to arrange them (by letter group) in a column on a *descending scale* from

> *most abstract (scientific)*
>> down to
> *most down to earth*

not forgetting that each word has to begin with the sound /saɪ/. Our own attempt (below),[2] matched up rather neatly with the source languages of the words concerned. This is, of course, a very subtle effect.

More obviously, there is a graphical element in the effect that a writer can achieve when (as often happens) there is a *choice* between words of similar meaning but from different source languages.

Some examples:[3]

from Anglo-Saxon	from Norman-French	from Latin
child		infant
job	employment	avocation
calling	vocation	
	career	
keen	diligent	sedulous
ghost	phantom	(spirit)
	spectre	
	spirit	
lift	elevate	
raise		
kind	type	species

More obviously still, there are spellings which associate strongly with certain areas of vocabulary.

Examples:

Initial X. (Greek / Hellenistic)	Xantippe
	Xerxes
	Xenophon
Diphthong. (Classical / Medical)	aesthetic
Formerly printed <œ> <æ>	anaesthetic
	mediaeval
	oesophagus
	amoeba
	oestrus
	oedema
	haemophilia
	haemorrhage
Terminal <-on> (Particle physics)	ion
Pronounced /ɒn/	photon
	positron
	electron
	neutron
	muon
Initial <kn>	knock
(Rather homespun words of German origin)	knee
	knickers
	knackers
	knave
	knife
	knit
	knot
	knuckle
	knead

(ii) Sometimes the *graphic* level 'helps out' the *phonic* level by giving different spellings to words that sound the same (homophones).

no	know	need	knead
gays	gaze	bred	bread
beat	beet	awl	all
ore	oar, or	taught	taut, tort
night	knight	mite	might
write	rite, right	not	knot
wade	weighed	paw	pour, poor, pore
bawd	board, bored, baud		

and so forth

This differentiation (which would have to be sacrificed in a 'reformed' or 'phonetic' alphabet) makes life difficult for spellers but is clearly functional for fluent reading. A recent treatment (Albrow, 1972) puts it like this; 'Plurality of symbolisation . . . should be seen as useful in the written medium in that it provides visual differentiation between words in a situation where clues to meaning are likely to be lacking when compared to the clues or opportunities for clarification which obtain in the spoken situation.' We may remind ourselves that *the first duty of a <word> is to look different from other <words>*.

c. *Graphic/phonic* levels inform the level of *syntax* (grammar).

i. The writing system labels certain words as 'grammatical' by spelling them with *only two letters* whereas 'ordinary' words are never spelled with less than three. Grammatical words are words which function only as indicators of grammatical function or structure as opposed to 'contextual' or lexical words which refer to objects or activities of the ordinary world. Thus *to* would be regarded as a grammatical word while *gerbil* would be a contextual or lexical word. Other words labelled as grammatical by their spelling are

is
he
if
as
an

It follows that when a lexical word sounds the same as a grammatical word it has to be given an additional letter to indicate its status, thus

grammatical	*lexical*
be	bee
we	wee

in	inn
or	oar
so	sew

(ii) A group of words that are related grammatically (they are demonstratives or 'pointers') are also related phono/graphically in that they begin with <*th*> pronounced \ð\ (a combination that only occurs initially in grammatical words), so:

this, that, these, those, the

Some other grammatical words which are 'marked' in this way are

thus, there, thence, thither

Similarly, initial <wh-> (variously pronounced) marks a group of questioning words that *do not* permit the answer 'yes' or 'no'.

	('Are you going out?'	'Yes.' 'No.'
but	'*When* are you going out?'	'Later on.')

Interestingly, these <wh->, words' are broadly related to some of the '<th->' words' discussed above, so

when?	then
where?	there
whence?	thence
whither?	thither
which?	this, that, these, those
who? whom?	they, them
whose?	theirs
(how)	thus

Proper nouns (names) are marked in the graphology by initial capitals. When they coincide with another kind of word they are often distinguished by a *doubled consonant letter*.

lad	Ladd
hog	Hogg
stubs	Stubbs

pit	Pitt
pen	Penn
man	Mann
web	Webb[4]

Summing-up on Redundancy

The preceding sections on redundancy have examined the ways in which the four modes or channels contained in the written signal can act in concert to maintain the flow of information necessary for fast reading. These sources of information are just as much available to slow readers and dyslexic readers as they are to fluent readers, but special help will be needed to see that they are understood and utilised as effectively as possible.

In the concluding sections we consider in some detail the information that is carried by the *syntactic channel*.

Notes

[1]   Text here means a stretch of written language (anything from a sentence to a novel) with which a reader is engaged.

[2]

More scientific/abstract

	psi-onics	
Graeco/Roman	psy-chiatry, psy-chotic	↑
	cy-press, cy-bernetics	
	cy-clotron	
Romance	sci-ence, sci-entology	
	ci-der, ci-te	
	sig-n	
Anglo-Saxon	si-de, si-dle	↓
	sigh, sigh-t	

More down to earth/everyday

[3]   Etymologies are from Skeat, *Etymological Dictionary of the English Language*, Oxford 1882

[4]   Much of the discussion in this and surrounding sections draws on 'The initial teaching of reading and writing' (1968) an influential paper by D. Mackay and B. Thompson, Schools Council Programme in Linguistics and English Teaching, Longman. One has to regret their assertion (p. 36) that 'letters obviously cannot "say" anything'.

Chapter 3
Syntactic information: prediction

'The coming grammatical scheme'

By *prediction* we mean the *foreknowledge* that a reader has of a text as a piece of language. We claim that this foreknowledge is an indispensable ingredient of fluent reading (and listening).

Prediction arises in two separate, but closely related, ways.

1. Long-range prediction

A reader already knows *in advance* a substantial part of the whole content of any possible text or message because he or she knows that it will be structured in accordance with the grammatical rules of some language. (For our purposes the language will be English.) These rules are stored in the reader's mind ready to be activated and applied to the interpretation of a message. At short range (see next section), they are triggered by 'grammatical' cues contained (one could say 'hidden') in the text. In much the same way, one could say that a television set is able to keep up with the shifting studio scene because it 'knows' in advance that any picture it has to decode will have been scanned in an interlacing pattern at a rate of 625 scans per second. This and much more 'grammatical' information is stored in the television set and is activated and maintained by signals invisible to the viewer.

Although 'grammatical' knowledge is essentially automatic and internalised, it is partly accessible and can be taught/learned to some extent as when someone learns to read or understand a foreign language.

Without such grammatical knowledge, fluent reading, or for that matter fluent listening, would not be possible.

2. Short-range prediction

A reader has advance knowledge at short range of the *specific* content of a particular text. This knowledge is activated and delivered through the combination of optical and linguistic effects noted at the beginning of Book Three and it extends only a short distance ahead of the focus of attention. This capability again depends on 'grammatical' or 'syntactic' properties of written language which can be, and for the dyslexic must be, partly taught. Syntactic aids to prediction will be considered at length in the next sections.

Readers who find the concept of *linguistic foreknowledge* difficult, fanciful or objectionably novel may be interested to learn that similar ideas were propounded with admirable clarity and force by the American psychologist E.B. Huey in a book published as long ago as 1908.1 Two extracts are printed below (with our emphases).

Huey's insights are the more remarkable in that they were arrived at without benefit of modern linguistic theory and modern computer technology, both of which make it very easy to entertain the idea of stored grammatical knowledge.[2]

> Our words are thoroughly organised according to [the] *general associative habits of our language* and when any given series has occurred in our reading the sort of words and sentence forms that belong in sequence with these are *subexcited in advance of their appearance on the page and need but slight cues from the page to cause them to spring into perceptual consciousness.* (p. 142)
>
> [Even when] the phrase or sentence has never occurred in our reading before in exactly its present wording, the inner readiness for it is almost as complete: and it will inwardly complete itself from a few visual clues if . . . its words and parts of speech stand in familiar grammatical sequences so that each associatively helps the other to rise and remain in consciousness. (p. 143)

Syntactic Functions in Reading: Preliminary Survey

We shall treat as 'syntactic'[3] all those linguistic patterns and structures which are important for '*prediction*'. Three main topics which will be covered in detail are briefly summarised here: syllable and stress; word structure; and sentence structure.

1. Syllable and stress

We know in advance that words will fit into a sound pattern made up of *syllables,* of which some will be more heavily *weighted* (stressed) than others. For instance, serendipity (/sɛrəndɪpətɪ/) contains five syllables

1	2	3	4	5
sɛ	rən	dɪ	pə	tɪ

of which the most heavily weighted is   dɪ

2. Word structure

We know in advance that words will often be divisible into smaller elements (*word fragments*) which contribute *in some way* to the total meaning of the word and which have their own separate existence in the life of the language.

For instance, the word *villains* contains two elements of structure
(*villain* | *s*)
of which the first means 'wicked person' and the second means 'more than one'.

Villain and *s* are meaningful in the ordinary sense of the word (Type 1).

Similarly, the word *villainous* contains two elements of structure
(*villain* | *ous*)
of which the first means 'wicked person' (the ordinary kind of meaning) while the second *permits* the quality of wickedness to be applied to some person or thing as in a *villainous expression*. The meaning of *-ous* lies in *what it does* (Type 2).

Similarly again, if one considers the words
conceive, perceive, receive, deceive
it becomes apparent that they each contain two elements

con | *ceive   per* | *ceive   re* | *ceive   de* | *ceive*

of which one (-ceive) is common to all four words and has no particular meaning while con- per- re- and de- (also meaningless [4]) are able to combine with -ceive to form the basis of a series of units that are meaningful. In this series the meaning of items like con-, per-, re-, and de- lies in their ability (in conjunction with items like -ceive) to *permit* and *distinguish* different units to which meaning can be attached (Type 3).

3. Sentence structure

We know in advance that words will be ordered in a way that simultaneously reflects and activates their grammatical potential.
For instance

> *dog bites man and*
> *man bites dog*

are not identical in meaning even though the words are the same.

The effect of word order is enhanced by the *labelling* effect of word fragments discussed in the previous section:

> a brilliant act|or act|s brilliantly

In the remaining chapters we look in greater detail at the three syntactic functions outlined above.

---

[1] *The Psychology and Pedagogy of Reading* by Edmund Burke Huey. (References are to the MIT Press edition of 1968.) Huey refers extensively to the thinking of the philosopher William James and in particular to his *Psychology (Advanced course)* (Henry Holt, 1892). It is sometimes difficult – and perhaps not necessary in the present context – to separate out the contributions made by each of these writers.

[2] The linguistic theory referred to here derives from the work of F. de Saussure (1916) and A.N. Chomsky (see, for instance, *Syntactic Structures,* 1957).

[3] The term *syntactic* is here given a much wider range than is customary and really means 'those aspects of linguistic organisation that are not semantic.' In an expository text it seems well worth avoiding an elaboration of phonological and morphological terminology.

[4] The fact that con-, per-, re-, de-, had meanings in earlier stages of the romance languages is irrelevant since these meanings do not apply to present day uses of English.

Chapter 4
Syllable and stress: more about syntactic features

Basic facts

1. Syllables are features of *speech*.
2. Syllables carry stress and are therefore *rhythmical*.
3. Syllabic rhythms play a part in *prediction*.
4. Syllabic rhythms are important for *spelling*.
5. Stress can *shift*.

1. Syllables are a feature of speech [1]

When people are talking they do not produce sounds in a smoothly modulated flow such as might be emitted by a talkative vacuum cleaner, but rather they produce a string of mini-utterances or *syllables* which follow one another in rapid and rhythmical succession (more like the pop-pop-popping of a motor boat). Each syllable is felt as a single articulatory movement and can therefore be said on a single beat or finger tap. This fact explains and underlies the rhythmic potential both of verse and of ordinary speech. The rhythmic potential of syllables is reinforced by *stress*.

2. Syllables are carriers of stress

Typically, a spoken /syllable/ consists of a vowel *sound* which may be preceded and/or followed by one or more consonant *sounds*.[2]

So, we can have words of

one syllable

I	/a͟ɪ/
straps	/st͟ræps/

196

two syllables

poppy /pɒ-pɪ/

three syllables

popular /pɒ-pjʊ-lə/

four syllables

population /pɒ-pjʊ-leɪ-ʃn̩/

five syllables

popularity /pɒ-pjʊ-læ-rə-tɪ/

and so on.

In every case where a single word is spoken *in isolation* (as in the examples above), there will be one syllable which is felt to be more 'weighty' than the others.[3] Such a syllable is said to be 'stressed'. *The stressed syllables* are underlined in the examples above.

At this point, readers should test their perception of syllable and stress by noting down the number of syllables (taps) in each of the following words. They should also indicate which syllable is carrying the heaviest stress. The simplest way to do this will be by marking the vowel letter in the stressed syllables.

First test. (Cover right hand column)

tadpole	[two syllables. Stress on the first syllable.		
		tadpole	/tædpəʊl/]
elephant	[three –	elephant	/eləfn̩t/]
pig	[one –	pig	/pɪg/]
hippopotamus	[five –	hippopotamus	/hɪpəpɒtəməs/
rhinoceros	[four –	rhinoceros	/raɪnɒsərəs/

Second test. (Cover right hand column)

tiger	[two –	tiger	/taɪgə/
centipede	[three –	centipede	/sentəpid]
yellowhammer	[four –	yellowhammer	/jeləʊhæmə/
tyrannosaurus	[five –	tyrannosaurus	/tɪrænəsɔrəs/
cat	[one –	cat	/kæt/

When words are strung together in speech the alternation of strongly
and weakly stressed syllables gives rise to a rhythmic pulsation in the
spoken sentence which sometimes overrides the stress pattern of the
individual words. This feature is most obvious in verse, but it occurs
in ordinary speech as well. Its particular fascination for small children provides a useful lever for teaching purposes.

> <u>Hi</u>ckory, <u>di</u>ckory, <u>dock</u>,
> The <u>mouse</u> ran <u>up</u> the <u>clock</u>,
> The <u>clock</u> struck <u>one</u>,
> The <u>mouse</u> ran <u>down</u>,
> <u>Hi</u>ckory, <u>di</u>ckory, <u>dock</u>.

An 'ordinary language' example would be

<u>Which</u> is the <u>train</u> to <u>Crewe</u>, <u>please?</u> [4]

Readers may find it helpful to say the above examples aloud while
maintaining a steady finger tap on each underlined syllable.

3. Syllabic rhythms play a part in prediction

We have seen that syllable and stress together invest words with
rhythm which is then carried forward into the rhythmic and melodic
flow of spoken language.

The ability to anticipate and participate in this patterning no
doubt contributes in an important way to our foreknowledge
of spoken language, which in turn accounts for our otherwise mysterious ability to keep up with, and even move ahead of, what is being
said even when the subject-matter is quite unfamiliar and novel.

This aspect of spoken language has its analogue in written
language as well so that the reader is required to develop the linguistic insights needed to detect graphic clues to imminent rhythmical
and structural interactions. <Words> have to be approached not as
undifferentiated lumps, but as organisations of stressed and
unstressed syllables so that, for instance, a fluent reading of

<repellently>

demands that it be scanned as a structure in which the stressed syllable
-*pell*- acts both as a rhythmic focus and as a structural peg on which
to hang the (unstressed) word fragments

re-
-ent
-ly

The spikiness of the consonant letters no doubt plays its part in this necessary prefiguring of <repellently> by sketching in a rough demarcation of syllable boundaries.

It can be noted in conclusion that good teaching practice already embodies some of the insights discussed above – for instance, the use of finger taps as a way of identifying syllabic patterns in written language by reference to the rhythms of speech; one can mention also the well-established principle that every <syllable> will contain a <vowel>.

4. Syllabic rhythms are important for spelling

At this point we should review the notion of the *symbol/sound relationship*, emphasising in particular that the relationship works in two directions. Notoriously, English graphology employs multiple relationships in both directions. This is particularly the case when the symbol or sound is a vowel.

For example.

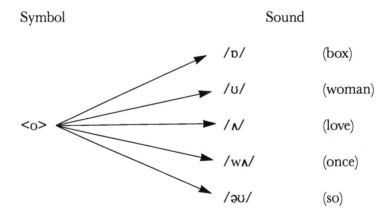

Symbol	Sound	
	/ɒ/	(box)
	/ʊ/	(woman)
<o>	/ʌ/	(love)
	/wʌ/	(once)
	/əʊ/	(so)

and so forth. Similarly

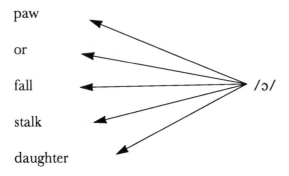

paw

or

fall   /ɔ/

stalk

daughter

The sounds in the right-hand column (upper diagram) can be referred to as different *values* of the letter <o>. The letters in the left-hand column (lower diagram) can be referred to as different *equivalences* of the sound /ɔ/.

Nevertheless, and despite the multiplicity of values and equivalences which certainly occur, there are still (as we have seen) important regularities in the English writing system which have to be mastered and internalised by the learning reader. Some of the most useful of these are bound up with *syllable structure*.

The principles involved are best illustrated by considering some <words> ('nonsense words') that happen *not* to occur in English but for which our internalised knowledge of spelling rules will still supply a plausible pronunciation. ('Real' applications of the rules are added in brackets.)

Presented with <*vad*> it is safe to assume that most readers would respond with /væd/ (like *lad*, and unlike *wad*) in accordance with the general principles given in Book Three, Chapter 1.

Similarly <*vade*> would be read aloud as /veɪd/ (like *wade*). The silent <e> enforces a 'long' reading of <a> again in accordance with very well-known principles. However when one tries to build up the imaginary word by the addition of a word fragment [5] like <*er*> or <*ing*>, then difficulties begin to arise.

The nonsense word <*vader*> will probably be read as /veɪdə/ (like *wader*). It appears that the <e> in <-er> still exerts a *lengthening effect* on the <a> of <vad>, even though

1. It is in a different syllable
2. It is no longer silent

Similarly, *<vading>* is most likely to be read as /veɪdɪŋ/
(like *lading*). It seems that, in this situation, the *lengthening
effect* of silent <e> can also be supplied by the letter <i>
and that <e> can be dispensed with altogether;
<vading> preserves the 'long' value without the need
for <vadeing>. So far, so good. But supposing one
wants to build the fragments -er and -ing on to the
imaginary word *<vad>* (/væd/)?
<vader>, and <vading> will still be interpreted
('wrongly') as /veɪdə/ and /veɪdɪŋ/ when what we
wanted to arrive at was /væbə/ and /vædɪŋ/.

The English writing system solves this problem with an ingenious
and purely graphical device, by doubling the intervening consonant
letter to produce

vadder (like *ladder*)
vadding (like *cladding*)

In this way, the letter <a> is *insulated* from the lengthening effect of
the following vowel letter and can preserve its 'short' value giving the
desired sound–symbol equivalence <a> = /æ/.

What we are describing here is a rather rare phenomenon in the
English writing system – a spelling rule without exceptions. The first
vowel letters in for instance:

cladding
bedding
bidding
nodding
budding

will *always* be read with the 'short' values and *never* with the 'long'
values. Notice, however, that the rule only applies when the consonant has been doubled *at the syllable boundary*. If it was double to begin
with, as in

tall
wall
call

then no doubling can take place at the syllable boundary and the
<a> retains the same 'long' value (/ɔ/) in both positions

taller
walling
caller

The reverse rule (vowels have long values before single consonant letters) *does* have exceptions – for example, polish, radish, credit, punish.

What has to be emphasised here is that we are dealing with a powerful and invariable rule of English spelling which is *dependent on syllable structure*. The addition of an extra syllable brings into operation spelling rules which influence sound–symbol relations in a regular way. Compare our automatic response to

diggest	and	digest
'sillent'		silent
canning		caning
fatter		fatal
silly		silage

and so forth.

It is interesting that this rule is a writing device merely. The *pronunciation* of the consonant letter remains the same whether it is single or double. Other syllable-related spelling rules tend to reflect features of the spoken language.

Of these, the most general is the rule that the vowel letter *in a stressed syllable* tends to have the value that it would have in a monosyllable: in other words, the spelling of the *stressed syllable* tends to follow the rules described in Chapter 1.[6]

The converse of this rule is also of considerable importance in English. It states that when a syllable is *unstressed*, the rules governing the relationship between vowel letter and vowel sound will often, though not always, be different from the rules that apply in monosyllables. This comes about because the *pronunciation* of a /syllable/ often changes when it ceases to carry stress, while the *spelling* of the corresponding <syllable> remains the same. If, for instance, one considers the word

im*port*ance

it is clear that the *stressed* syllable -port- is pronounced and spelled like the monosyllable *port*, whereas the *unstressed* syllable -ance, although it is still *spelled* as in the monosyllables *chance* or *dance* is now pronounced quite differently. (/əns/) instead of /ɑns/ or /æns/). The value of <a> has changed from /ɑ/ to /ə/.

To put it another way, the correct reading/spelling of *-ance* depends on its status as a stressed or unstressed syllable. To put it another way still, English has a different spelling *system* for stressed and unstressed syllables – the same spelling represents a different sound. This comes out particularly clearly in cases where there is *movement of stress.*

5. Stress can shift

We have seen that the letter <a> has two primary values in mono-syllables being 'long' (/eɪ/) or 'short' (/æ/) according to circumstances. In the case of the word *fate*, the <a> has the long value before silent <e>. In the word *fatal* the first syllable is still stressed and so the letter <a> retains the same value that it had in the mono-syllable – (/feɪtl̩/). The second syllable of *fatal* (spoken) is unstressed and so the vowel sound is *reduced* to /ə/ or even swallowed up entirely in the pronunciation of /l̩/. Correspondingly, the second <a> of *fatal* (written) has a very different value from the first, or even no value at all.

Compare *naval, nasal, pagan.*

If one now considers the word *fatality* it can be seen (or rather heard) that the stress has shifted to the second syllable

(/fətæ,lətɪ/)

and the second <a> now has one of the values appropriate to a monosyllable – the 'short' /æ/ in this case – while the first <a> now has the reduced value /ə/.

<f a t a l i t y>
/f ə t æ l ə t ɪ/

Compare   *person*   *personify*
               personal   *personality*

An even clearer example is provided by words like *present* and *frequent*, where an alteration of stress is solely responsible for allocation of meaning and grammatical function. In these two cases the vowel letter <e> is involved.

For instance, <present> can represent *either*

> *pre*sent   ('Christmas present'), a noun, *or*
> pre*sent*   ('She will present the prizes'), a verb,

the change of meaning being accomplished in the spoken language by a shift of stress (/preznt/ to /prəzent/) while the written version remains unaltered. In each case the <e> in the stressed syllable has the 'monosyllabic' value (/ɛ/), while in the unstressed syllable it has a 'reduced' value. (/ə/, /ɪ/ or nothing at all.)

Readers may like to work out the sound/symbol relations in *fre*quent/*frequent* for themselves.

Interweaving of Levels

We have encountered three types of phenomenon in our discussion of reading and *stress shift*;

1	syllable/stress	*fa*tal v fa*ta*lity

2	word fragments	e.g. re-
		       -pell
		       -ent
		       -ly

3	sentence grammar	*pre*sent is a noun pre*sent* is a verb

This interrelation of levels is typical of language behaviour and of the way that linguistic insights have to be pressed into service in the reading process. *Word fragments* are further discussed in the next section. *Sentence grammar* is the subject of Chapter 6.

It will be convenient to deal here with another topic that spans more than one level, namely the effect that certain *word fragments* have in bringing about a shift of stress. This effect can be quite helpful in resolving blocks over spelling as when someone who has a blank spot about the spelling of *history* is helped by *historical* or when more sophisticated mis-spellers find that *existential* gives a useful clue to *existence*. Compare also *desperate, desperation; mystery, mysterious.*

A list of word fragments which have the effect of shifting stress (as well as changing grammatical status) is supplied below (column 2), together with a list of words that can be affected in this way (column 1).

1	2
formal, severe, principal popular	-ity
poet, magnet, majesty	-ic
courage, industry, conscience, mystery	-(i)ous
family	-ar
moderate, private, machine, separate, desperate	-ion
major, peculiar, similar, necessary, neutral, total	-ity
experiment, increment, consonant, incident, medicine	-al
medicine, method, hysteria, category, history, philosophy	-(i)cal
refer, prefer, recur	-ence
comedy, flying saucer	-ian

(This category is further considered from a grammatical standpoint in Chapter 6.)

Conclusion

We have discussed syllable and stress at length and in detail because of their fundamental role in spoken and written language and because they are frequently referred to in introductory texts and manuals without any full explanation. They also underlie the topics dealt with in the remainder of this book.

Notes

[1]   This treatment regards *syllable* as an indivisible unit. However, a good deal of attention has recently focused on a subdivision of the syllable into the constituents onset and rime. This work is mainly due to Rebeccah Treiman (e.g. Treiman, 1985) and Usha Goswami (e.g. Goswami, 1988, 1990). Goswami gives the following example (Snowling and Thomson, 1991, Chapter 8):

trip   =   /t/ - /r/ - /ɪ/ - /p/   (linear analysis by successive phonemes)

trip   =   syllable   (hierarchical analysis by syllable constituents)

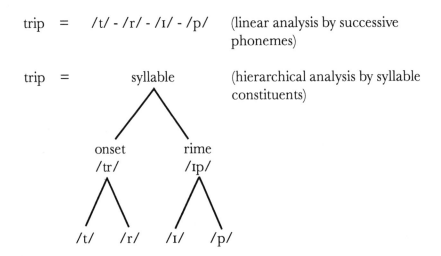

The rime corresponds to the vowel phoneme of the syllable and anything that follows it. The onset corresponds to anything that precedes the vowel phoneme. There is evidence to suggest that children make use of both onset and rime when they come to analyse written words. For discussion see Goswami in Snowling and Thomson,1991. 'The implications of intrasyllabic knowledge for handicap (backwardness) in reading are currently only beginning to be explored.'

[2]   Similarly, in the written language one can say that every <syllable> contains a *vowel letter* (or digraph) although not necessarily in the expected position
<rat | tle>

[3]   Of course, in monosyllables the single syllable will be 'weighted'.

[4]   Example from Abercrombie (1967).

[5]   Word fragments are discussed at length in Chapter 5.

[6]   In fact, the consonant doubling rule that we have just been discussing could be regarded as a special case of this rule – in other words as a way of guaranteeing that in the circumstances there described the vowel letter in the stressed syllable *retains its monosyllabic value.*

Chapter 5
Word fragments

In the last section we examined the way in which spoken words are built up from smaller speech units (*syllables*) with important consequences both for reading and for spelling. This section deals with a different but no less significant way of building words, out of units which we shall be calling *word fragments*.

The difference consists in the fact that syllables are units of sound, merely, *with no meaning associations* whereas word fragments always contribute *in some way* to the total meaning of a word. This is not to say that word fragments are always meaningful in the ordinary sense (though they often are).

Three types of word fragment can be distinguished.

Type one fragments

Sometimes word fragments are meaningful in much the same way that *words* are meaningful.

Example 1. *dis trust ful*
This word contains three fragments;
a. -trust- which has the meaning it would have as a separate word,
b. dis-   which means something like opposite
c. -ful   which means full of

So the meaning of distrustful is something like an addition sum made up from the meaning of the constituent fragments

   distrustful = (*full of*) + (*the opposite of*) + (*trust*).

Example 2. *Villain s*
   villain - = evil person (a 'word meaning')

-s = more than one (a 'grammatical meaning')
So *villains* can also be treated as an addition sum,

villains = (*more than one*) + (*evil person*).

While it is possible for an element to be *both a word fragment and a sylla-ble-* (for instance *dis-,* above) – it is important to remember that frag-ments and syllables are *different kinds of unit* and not necessarily co-extensive. For instance, in the example above, the word fragment *villain* is *more* than one syllable long, while the word fragment *-s* is *less* than one syllable long.

'Type one' fragments are frequently used consciously or uncon-sciously in the construction of new words. For instance in

deactivate, decontaminate, deodorant, destabilise, retro-rocket, retro-active,

de- and *retro-* both mean something like '*reverse*'.
Compare also stress-ful, dis-educate.

Type two fragments

The meaning of a 'type two' fragment is what it *does* or *permits.*

Example 1. *Villain ous.*
Villain- is still a 'type one' fragment but *-ous* is 'type two': it *permits* the quality 'evil person' to be *applied* adjectivally to some person or thing as in *a villainous expression.*

Example 2. *villain y*
Similarly, the fragment *-y* in *villain y* isolates the quality that makes an evil person evil and allows one to speak of it in the abstract.

Example 3. *victim is ation*
victim- ('exploited person') is a 'type one' fragment, while -ise (type 2) – *permits* one to energise the concept 'exploited person' and employ it as a verb in a sentence. So '*victim-ise*' = (turn someone into) (an exploited person).
-ation – *permits* this activity to be reinstated as a noun and given the meaning appropriate to that grammatical role.[1]

So, *victimisation* will be (*the act of*) (*turning someone into*) (*an exploited person*)

Type two fragments are also used in the formation of new words with an awareness (at some level) of their function, e.g. *privat is ation*. Notice that word fragments often adapt their spelling to their position in a larger formation, as with the two 'missing e's' in *privat(e)is(e)ation*.

Type three fragments

'Type three fragments' have no meaning at all as individual units. Their function is to act as building blocks from which words can be constructed in a way that is systematic and therefore recognisable and therefore predictable. Meaning can then be attached to the whole resulting word (see D. Bolinger, *Aspects of Language, 1968*, p. 56). Examples. Words like *per ceive, re ceive, de ceive* contain two units which both appear to lead an independent existence in the life of the language.

for instance *per-, re-, de-*, are found in

perform	reverse	desist
perforate	resist	delay
permit	reply	deride
perverse		

and so forth, while *-ceive* occurs in *receive, deceive, conceive.*

None of these items is separately meaningful. For instance it is not possible to attach a particular meaning to *re-* or *-ceive* in *receive*. Nonetheless, they are clearly word fragments which have somehow to be brought within the scope of our statement that word fragments 'always contribute in some way to the meaning of the total word'.

How can what is meaningless contribute to meaning? The answer appears to be that fragments like

-ceive	(conceive)
-mit	(submit)
-spire	(aspire)
-sist	(insist)
-pose	(suppose)

are 'empty' items which the language has at its disposal for the formation of words.[2]

The very large number of these items which will be needed for word building can be still further increased by combining them with a number of equally arbitrary 'tags' (*de-*,[3] *pro-*, *re-*, and so on) to give rise to a wide range of different words to which meanings can then be attached.

Type three fragments, to put it briefly, lack *meaning* but possess *function* in that they permit the construction of words from recognisable (and therefore predictable) units.

Although type three fragments are less frequently used in building new formations than are fragments of the other types new 'type three' formulations do occur as for instance: transistor, transceiver.

Some General Observations about Word Fragments

1. Word fragments can alter their substance (spelling/pronunciation) while continuing to make the same contribution to the meaning of the total word. Some examples

> pro*ceed*, pro*ceed*ings but pro*cess*ion
> repeats, repeatedly but repetition, repetitive
> receive, perceive but reception, perception

Just as it is helpful in reading to perceive words themselves as structural entities rather than as unanalysed lumps of language, so skilful reading and language use will be further helped by introducing and strengthening the insight that words have familial relationships with other words, some of which are not obvious at first sight.

2. *Fragment collision, fragment junction*

Similar insights are called into play in cases where a historical collision of fragments has lead to a pronunciation/spelling change. Historical considerations *are* relevant in such cases because the traces they leave help to explain present day spellings. Some examples:

The type one fragment *in-*, meaning 'not', was melded into other fragments at an earlier stage of the language; the junction is now marked by a spelling change

intestate	(in-testate: no change)
innumerable	(in-numerable: no change but explains doubling of the <n>,)
irreligious	(in-religious, <n-r> becomes <rr>)
improbable	(in-probable, <n-p> becomes <m-p>)

Other cases of fragment junction have not brought about an obvious change in spelling but they help to explain consonant doublings that have come about 'naturally'. Thus:

dis-appear	=	disappear (no doubling, but)
dis-satisfied	=	dissatisfied
dis-solve	=	dissolve

and

clever-ly	=	cleverly (no doubling, but)
formal-ly	=	formally
total-ly	=	totally

and so on.

It is interesting to note that we have now encountered *five* ways in which the doubling of consonant letters (a minor but constant vexation of English spelling) can arise and be explained.

In monosyllables

    a. They are added to two letter words to save the rule that only 'grammatical' words can be spelt with fewer than three letters – in...inn.

    b. Doubling sometimes occurs when ordinary nouns are used as proper names:
man...Mann
stubs...Stubbs

In polysyllables

    c. Consonant letters are doubled to preserve the 'short' values of vowel letters when these might otherwise be lost. (Or to save the rule that vowel letters in stressed syllables retain the values that they would have in monosyllables.)
top...topping (not *toping*)
bit...bitter (not *biter*).

    d. Doubling may occur initially in the syllable to mark a historical junction of fragments:
approach, approve, apply, acclaim

    e. Doubling may occur across syllable boundaries where fragments happen to begin and end with identical letters.
dis-solve, normal-ly

3. Some useful terminology

The reading of polysyllabic words (and of any connected text) will be helped by

    a. a developing sense of their rhythmical patterning as reflected in the placement of stress

    b. a developing sense of their internal structure expressed in the relation between constituent fragments.

The following terminology is in common use for classifying constituents.

Fragments are subdivided into

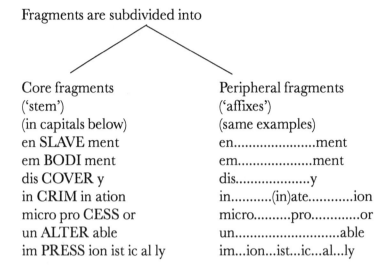

Core fragments	Peripheral fragments
('stem')	('affixes')
(in capitals below)	(same examples)
en SLAVE ment	en......................ment
em BODI ment	em...................ment
dis COVER y	dis...................y
in CRIM in ation	in..........(in)ate............ion
micro pro CESS or	micro..........pro.............or
un ALTER able	un............................able
im PRESS ion ist ic al ly	im...ion...ist...ic...al...ly

Core fragments give the impression of being the focus or starting-point for the word. Their meaning, when they have one, is often 'contextual' rather than 'grammatical'. They are sometimes referred to as the *stem or root* of the word and this horticultural metaphor seems appropriate in cases where the growth of a word can be traced in the contemporary language, as with:

ACT

ENACT

RE-ENACT

RE-ENACT MENT

RE-ENACT MENT S

There is a tendency, as here, for the core fragment to carry main stress, although the stress is sometimes shifted to other positions.

It seems reasonable to conjecture that effective knowledge of English and hence fluent reading will incorporate some sense of a building-up process at work in longer words and also a contrary sense of longer words as having constituent parts that are arranged on some plan; as, for instance, with

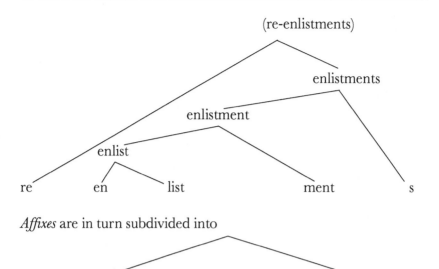

Affixes are in turn subdivided into

prefixes   and   suffixes
(attached before the core)   (attached after the core)
pre-fix   hope-*ful*
un-plug   clear-*ly*
fore-warn   cub-*ism*

Sometimes two core fragments are attached to each other by a process called *compounding* in order to form a new word or *compound*,

> e.g.   blackbird
> sunset
> hogshead
> push-button
> disk-drive
> somewhat

Compounds can carry affixes,

> tonguelash-ing
> heatseek-ing
> woodcutt-er

Compounds tend to start life as separate words, become hyphenated, and finally enter the vocabulary as single words,

> rat race, rat-race, ratrace

Stress-shift, word fragments, syllables

Although fragments and syllables operate at different levels of language they are (like everything else in language) highly interactive. In pointing out the tendency for core fragments to carry main stress we have already drawn attention to one kind of interchange between levels.

A further interaction takes place between

> stress patterning
> word fragments
> sentence grammar.[4]

A clear instance of this is the effect of *stress shift* in highlighting the presence of a *suffix* which allows a word to perform a different *sentence function.*

In the following examples we have underlined the syllable that is carrying main stress.

c<u>e</u>lebrate (verb)	becomes	cele<u>b</u>rity (noun)
<u>mo</u>ment (noun)		mo<u>men</u>tous (adjective)
<u>pos</u>sible (adjective)		possi<u>bili</u>ty (noun)
<u>i</u>rritate (adjective)		irri<u>ta</u>tion (noun)
<u>i</u>rritable (adjective)		irrita<u>bili</u>ty
<u>cou</u>rage (noun)		cou<u>ra</u>geous (adjective)
<u>per</u>sonal (adjective)		perso<u>na</u>lity (noun)
pre<u>fer</u> (verb)		<u>pre</u>ference (noun)
<u>par</u>liament (noun)		parlia<u>men</u>tary (adjective)
		parliamen<u>ta</u>rian (noun)

In a familiar manner the new function is both *signalled and enabled* by a syntactic change.

Notes

[1] The parts of speech and their sentence functions are discussed in Chapter 6.

[2] All these items and many others like them were meaningful in earlier source languages. The historical processes by which they became available to English are a fascinating subject for anyone with an interest in etymology, but are not present to the minds of everyday users and learners of the functioning language.

[3] What appears to be the 'same' fragment can function as more than one 'type'. Compare de- on pp. 206–7.

[4] To be further discussed in the next chapter.

Chapter 6
Sentence structure

Introduction

We *know in advance* that words will be arranged in a way that simultaneously bestows, reflects and activates their grammatical potential. This section continues and concludes our study of the ways in which written language is organised so as to provide the reader with the necessary flow of syntactic or *predictive* information which, in turn, will allow accompanying semantic or *contextual* information to be processed at high speed. This dual content is very clearly visible both in the internal *composition* and in the external *organisation* of words. At the level of *sentence structure* we shall be concerned with words as objects which the language

    1. *classifies* and
    2. *places in a certain order*

so as to make sentences.

Both these processes build on the reader's strong, but mainly unconscious, preconception of *word function*. We are now to consider the nature of this aspect of a reader's foreknowledge of a text and the ways in which it is addressed by actual sentences.

Two kinds of word

When words are strung together to make sentences it becomes apparent that they fall into two different *types or categories* which can conveniently be labelled *lexical* and *grammatical*. In relation to our previous discussion, the term *lexical* corresponds broadly to semantic/contextual, and the term *grammatical* corresponds to syntactic/predictive. The two types of word differ from each other in several ways which need not be elaborated here. Essentially one can say that *lexical* words (like)

> *garden*
> *cleverly*
> *revolutionise*
> *nice*

refer *outward* from language and point towards the qualities, essences, objects and experiences which go to make up our inner life and our sense of the material universe.

On the other hand, *grammatical* words like

> *if*
> *so*
> *in*
> *was*
> *while*

seem to lack this *referential* function, but to operate instead *within* language as a device for organising *other words* into useful structures.

Other differences

Once this broad two-way division has been accepted, certain other identifying features become apparent. For instance:

*   lexical words tend to *carry stress* in spoken language and to be *long* (have many letters) in written language
*   grammatical words tend not to carry stress in spoken language and to be short (have few letters) in *written language.*

As a way of summarising the discussion so far, the reader is invited to use the information given above in order to sort the seven words of the following partial sentence into the two types – lexical words (4); grammatical words (3).

While shepherds watched their flocks by night... [1]

However, for present purposes, the most important distinction to be made between lexical and grammatical words is that a lexical word has also a *grammatical coloration* and can be assigned to one of four *lexical parts of speech* as with the following example:

broad	(adjective)
breadth	(noun)
broaden	(verb)
broadly	(adverb)

which allow it to assume different functions in sentences. Grammatical words do not have this capacity.

On occasions when the 'same' grammatical word appears to be performing different functions, as with the two occurrences of *to* in

> *I have to go to the concert*

it seems more correct to say that this is *not* an instance of the 'same' word performing different functions (as is evidently the case with *broad* and *broadly*) but rather that we are here dealing with two *different* words that happen to look and sound the same (like *compound* = a mixture, and *compound* = an enclosure).

There is an obvious and important analogy to be drawn between lexical *words* in sentence structure and core *fragments* in word structure, both of which tend to be referential and to carry main stress.

So, the (part) sentence

> *to spread a doctrine*

corresponds in a sort of way to the word

> *indoctrinate*

doctrine and *-doctrin-*, both having a referential/contextual function which is supported (in the part sentence) by the grammatical words *to* and *a*
and (in the word) by the affixes *in-* and *-ate*.

In these examples the *grammatical words* and the *affixes* are both keeping up a kind of syntactic 'running commentary' on the non-syntactic part of the text.

The function of the words *a* and *to* in the same example is evidently to supply clues to the grammatical status of the *associated lexical words*.

Thus, a single slot following

> *a* ____

is very likely to be occupied by a *noun*, while

> *to* ____

sets up strong expectations of a following *verb*.

It is true that *to* (the other kind of *to*) could also be followed by a noun

> I went to Spread   [a place called Spread]
> I gave it to Spread [a person called Spread]

but in such a case the noun would have to be a proper name and marked as such in the written language by a capital S. No doubt the persistence of initial capitals for proper nouns is ascribable to such considerations.

Analogously, there are *word fragments* that supply clues to the grammatical function of the total word, for instance

> -ise, -ate   suggest verb,
> -tion, -ism,   suggest noun,
> -ish, -est   suggest adjective,
> -ly   suggests adverb.

The further one proceeds with this kind of discussion, the more evident it becomes that the language (in both spoken and written modes) attaches very great importance to the grammatical classification of lexical words.

Basic facts about the Grammatical Categories of Words (traditionally known as the parts of speech)

1. In the historical study of grammar, it has been usual to identify eight parts of speech but there has been a good deal of disagreement as to the exact categories to be so labelled. (See, for instance, Michael, 1970.) For the purposes of the present discussion, the following list seems reasonable.

The lexical parts of speech	The grammatical parts of speech
Adjective Noun Verb Adverb	Pronoun Preposition Conjunction Article Particle

Our attention will be focused mainly on the *lexical* parts of speech.
2. For a lexical word to function in a sentence it has to be assigned to one of the lexical parts of speech.

This is done by adding appropriate syntactic information. When this information is inappropriate or insufficient, then the resulting sentence may be meaningless or ambiguous, as in the well-known cases of

> *ship sails tomorrow* and *nursing swans can be dangerous.*

The addition of further syntactic information removes the ambiguity:
> *the* ship sails tomorrow/ship *the* sails tomorrow
> nursing swans *is/are* dangerous

3. The English language employs four main techniques for conferring and proclaiming the grammatical status of lexical words

1. Structural change (using *word fragments*)
2. Grammatical words
3. Word order
4. Stress (in spoken language only).
(5. Somewhat marginally, there are two graphical devices which apply in written language only, namely
    a. Capital letters to mark proper nouns (John)
    b. Apostrophes to mark nouns in general when they are possessively related to other units of language (the people's, Peter's).

The fact that spoken language employs four methods of continuously classifying lexical words into the 'parts of speech', and written language at least three, is sufficient proof that the grammatical analysis of word function (often stigmatised as a pointless and even dangerous academic exercise) is something that language itself treats as a *communicative* device of the highest importance. The process unfolds continuously in three or four separate but interlocking modes and is therefore another instance of *redundancy.*

We shall now treat the four methods in turn beginning with

1. Structural change
For the purpose of this discussion it will be convenient to regard each *lexical* word as representing an underlying *idea* or *lexeme.*

Thus the words

broad, breadth, broaden and *broadly*

have in common the *idea* of

'amplitude' 'generous width'.

They thus share *the same contextual meaning* but have *different grammatical functions*, which are signalled by a change in their internal structure. Thus

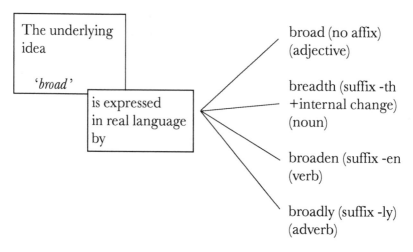

The underlying idea

'*broad*' is expressed in real language by

broad (no affix) (adjective)

breadth (suffix -th +internal change) (noun)

broaden (suffix -en (verb)

broadly (suffix -ly) (adverb)

Some sentences in which these functions occur:

1. As noun. 'The *breadth* of his imagination astounded them.'
2. As verb. 'We should now *broaden* the scope of our enquiry.'
3. As adjective. 'The *broad* sweep of his imagination astounded them.'
4. As adverb. 'He smiled *broadly*.'

The functions in greater detail:

Function 1. Noun. For naming ('*breadth*')
A word will be classified as a *noun* when it is naming or identifying some person, place or thing – in this case, the quality of being 'broad'.

Function 2. Verb. For energising ('*broaden*')
This function permits the underlying meaning to be energised or set

in motion. Words with this grammatical coloration will be classified as *verbs*. 'Broaden' will be the activity of making or becoming 'broad'.

Function 3. Adjective. For describing (1). *('broad')*.
The language finds it necessary to bring underlying meanings *into relationship with one another* in the way which is known grammatically as *describing*. Two parts of speech are provided for this purpose. When the meaning to be described has taken on the function *noun*, then the describing word will be called an *adjective*. Otherwise it will be called an *adverb*.
Example of adjectival function:

adjective   ⟶ noun
'The broad   sweep of his imagination astounded them.'

Function 4. Adverb. For describing (2) (*'broadly'*)
Like an adjective, an adverb is a *describing* function which brings a word into that relationship with other units. The other unit can be

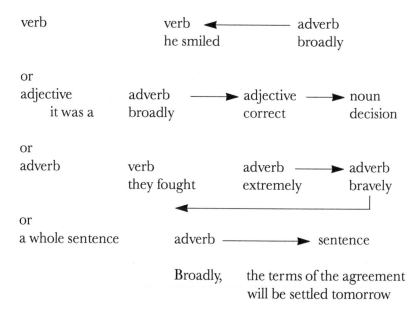

| verb | verb ⟵ adverb |
| | he smiled   broadly |

or
adjective   adverb ⟶ adjective ⟶ noun
     it was a   broadly   correct   decision

or
adverb   verb   adverb ⟶ adverb
    they fought   extremely   bravely
     ⟵——————————|

or
a whole sentence   adverb ⟶ sentence

       Broadly,   the terms of the agreement
                    will be settled tomorrow

It will be recalled that the preceding examples have been used to illustrate how words can be classified into different functions by means of a *structural change* (the addition or deletion of a word fragment), as with

broad, broaden, breadth, broadly

Before going on to consider other methods of conferring and signalling grammatical status, it may be helpful to supply some other examples of words that can 'switch' between different functions by means of a structural change.

Adjective (describe (1))	Verb (energise)	Noun (name)	Adverb (describe (2))
reactive reactionary	react	reaction	?reactively
long	lengthen	length	lengthily
kind kindly (a kindly act)	....	kindness	kindly (he spoke kindly)
universal	universalise	universe universality	universally
normal	normalise	normality	normally
restorative	restore	restoration	restoratively?
soft	soften	softness	softly
useful	use (/juz/)	use (/jus/)	usefully
formal	formalise	formality	formally

However, it must be emphasised that structural change alone is not sufficient to confer grammatical status. In any case it operates (in English) rather irregularly and untidily with numerous gaps and inconsistencies. Some instances of the 'gappiness' of structural change are given below.

adjective	noun	verb	adverb
polar	polarity pole polarisation	polarise	....
facile	facility	facilitate	?facilely
docile	docility	....	docilely
....	utility	utilise	....
....	debility	debilitate	....

Other ways of conferring grammatical status
Words can, and frequently do, switch functions *without making any corresponding structural change.* As a corollary one can note that the structure of a word often gives no indication of its grammatical status. For instance, it makes no sense to enquire about the 'part of

speech' or sentence function of

foul, limp or spare

considered in isolation, since they can each assume three different grammatical roles without structural change. However, once they are inserted in sentences their function becomes manifest.

We now provide a rather fuller list of words that have this property.

Adjective	*Verb*	*Noun*
foul	foul	foul
limp	limp	limp
top	top	top
spare	spare	spare
trim	trim	trim
right	right	right
slight	slight	slight
mute	mute	mute
wrong	wrong	wrong

Evidently, for words of this type, grammatical status is not assigned by structural change and it follows that different methods must be employed. It turns out that the continuous assignment of grammatical status is always done by at least two simultaneous and interactive processes. The second available method will be

2. Grammatical words

The operation of this technique is best seen by placing a lexical word in a number of contexts. We shall use for our example the 'invariable' lexical word *limp*

1.   He started to limp across the field. (*limp* is a verb)
2.   Jane was walking with a limp. (*limp* is a noun)
3.   They came up with a rather limp excuse. (*limp* is an adjective)

Clearly, the underlying meaning 'limp' is taking on different grammatical functions here and, equally clearly, the effect is achieved without structural change. Instead the work is done with the help of surrounding *grammatical words.*

In 1

to _____ labels *limp* as a verb.

In 2

with a _____ heralds a noun.

In 3

     *a rather*_____ _____ indicates the arrival of an adjective followed by a noun and *limp* is accordingly marked as an adjective.

We are dealing here with quite complex and subtle linguistic effects but it seems reasonable to suggest that the main function of *grammatical words* is to define the structure of sentences by providing redundant clues to the function of surrounding lexical words.

3. Word order

The examples above also illustrate how grammatical information is conveyed by *word order* or *position.*

     Thus in the sequence

       a rather _____ _____ _____

the *last* word is likely to be a noun and *intervening* words will be adjectives or adverbs:

       a rather surprisingly (adverb) clear (adjective) decision (noun)

     Of course, the insertion of a new *grammatical word* would change the situation:

a rather	*splendidly*	*lurid*	*way*	*to*	go.
	adv	adj	noun		verb

In the case of example 1 above

       he started to limp

the identification of *limp* as a verb is further assisted by its position after *started* (which is marked as a verb by its internal structure).

In the sequence

       he _____ed to _____

the likelihood that both slots will be filled by verbs is overwhelming.

a rather splendidly lurid way to go

shows all three techniques operating together;

word fragments	*-id* suggests <u>adjective</u> (morbid, rabid)
	-ly suggests <u>adverb</u> (splendidly)
grammatical words	*a, rather, to*
order/position	—as explained above, a sequence opened by *a rather* is likely to end in a noun, intervening words being adjectives or adverbs in that context. *to* ends the sequence.

We have now discussed three of the ways in which underlying meanings can manifest themselves as words in such a way as to declare and contribute their grammatical function in a particular sentence. Before proceeding to the last method, the reader might like to consider a few further examples. What function is each underlined word performing and how is it signalled?

1.   A <u>brilliant actor acts brilliantly</u>.
2.   The <u>speaker immediately abandoned his untenable position</u>.
3.   You can try to <u>explore</u> the <u>nearest planet</u>.
4.   We shall be <u>celebrating</u> the <u>inauguration</u> of the <u>robotic hyper-market</u>.
5.   They listened respectfully to his nonsensical observations and then forgot them <u>completely</u>.

4. Stress

This technique operates in the spoken and not in the written language but, like other aspects of the user's unconscious and antici-patory knowledge of language, it is no doubt brought to bear at *some* level of the reading process. Its most conspicuous contribution to sentence function lies in its ability *in isolation* to switch a number of lexical words from one grammatical role to another. The following is a selection from the words that can be affected in this way (stressed syllables underlined):

<u>pre</u>sents (things exchanged at Christmas) – a noun *becomes* pre<u>sents</u> (hands something over in a formal manner) – a verb.

progress (movement in a certain direction) – noun *becomes*
progress (to move in a certain direction) – a verb.

object (a thing) – a noun *becomes*
object (take exception to) – verb.

exports (noun) are what you export (verb)
a contest (noun) occurs when you contest something
(verb)
a suspect (noun) is someone you suspect (verb).

However, a more common use of stress in English is to highlight the effect of structural change. We have suggested elsewhere that these changes can sometimes be useful as aids to spelling. The next group of examples shows how *movement of stress* can go along with, and call attention to, a particular *word fragment*. The change of function is signalled and made operative by an interaction of these two elements.

celebrate (verb)	celebrity (noun)
moment (noun)	momentous (adjective)
possible (adjective)	possibility (noun)
irritate (verb)	irritation (noun)
irritable (adjective)	irritability (noun)
courage (noun)	courageous (adjective)
personal (adjective)	personality (noun)
prefer (verb)	preference (noun)
parliament (noun)	parliamentary (adjective)
	parliamentarian (noun)

Grammatical parts of speech
In conclusion, we give a brief account of the grammatical parts of speech together with a few examples.

Pronouns	Relate to participants in a discourse: *I, you, we, they, he, she, it*
Conjunctions	Connect portions of a text in various ways: *and, but, if, because*
Prepositions	Locate nouns in space and time: *before, under, through, beside*
Articles	Label nouns: *the, a, an*

Particles   Perform a variety of other labelling functions: e.g. *to* (in 'he wanted *to* go'); up (in 'he looked *up* the word')

Conclusion

This review of English sentence structure concludes our survey of the predictive devices available to users of written English, their nature and their interactions. It provides a sufficient basis for the teaching of literacy and we hope that it will also provide a challenge both to teachers, who may want to find ways of making these insights more accessible to their pupils, and to linguists who may want to make fresh discoveries in a new and still largely unexplored area.

Notes

[1] Answer: Lexical words are *shepherds, watched, flocks, night.* Grammatical words are while, their, by.

Bibliography

ABERCROMBIE, D. (1967). *Elements of General Phonetics*. Edinburgh: University Press.

ADULT LITERACY AND BASIC SKILLS UNIT (1983). *Literacy and Numeracy. Evidence from the National Child Development Study*. London: ALBSU.

ALBROW, K.H. (1972). *The English writing system: notes towards a description*. Schools Council Programme in Linguistics and English Teaching. Papers, Series 11, Volume 2. London: Longman.

BENTON, A.L. (1974). Developmental dyslexia: neurological aspects. In Friedlander, W.J. (Ed.) *Advances in Neurology*, Vol. 7. New York: Raven Press.

BENTON, A.L. AND PEARL, D. (Eds) (1978). *Dyslexia: an appraisal of current knowledge*. Oxford: Oxford University Press.

BISHOP, C. (1964). 'Transfer of word and letter training in reading'. *Journal of Verbal Learning and Verbal Behaviour*, **3**:215.

BODER, E. (1970). Developmental dyslexia: a diagnostic approach based on the identification of three sub-types. *Journal of School Health*, **40**: 289–298.

BODER, E. (1971). Developmental dyslexia: prevailing diagnostic concepts and a new diagnostic approach. In Myklebust, H. (Ed.) *Progress in Learning Disabilities*. New York: Grune and Stratton.

BOLINGER, D. (1968). *Aspects of Language*. New York: Harcourt, Brace and World.

BRITISH PSYCHOLOGICAL SOCIETY (1983). *Specific Learning Difficulties: the specific reading difficulty versus 'dyslexia' controversy resolved?* Division of Education and Child Psychology, Occasional Paper.

BULLOCK, A. (1975). *A Language for Life*. Report of the Committee of Inquiry into Reading and the Use of English. London: Department of Education and Science.

CHOMSKY, A.N. (1957). *Syntactic Structures*. The Hague: Mouton.

CHURCHILL, D.W. (1978). *The Language of Autistic Children*. London: V.H. Winton and Sons.

CLARK, M.M. (1976). *Young Fluent Readers*. London: Heinemann Educational Books.

COLTHEART, M. PATTERSON, K. AND MARSHAL, J. (1980). *Deep Dyslexia*. International Library of Psychology.

CRITCHLEY, M. (1970). *The Dyslexic Child*. London: Heinemann.

CROSBY, R. (1969). *Reading and the Dyslexic Child*. London: Souvenir Press.

CRYSTAL, D. (1976). *Child Language, Learning and Linguistics*. London: Edward Arnold.

DIACK, H. (1965). *In Spite of the Alphabet*. London: Chatto and Windus.

EDUCATION ACT (1981). *Special Educational Needs*. London: HMSO.

FILDES, L.G. (1921). A psychological inquiry into the nature of the condition known as congenital word blindness. *Brain*, **44**; 286–307.

FLESCH, R. (1981). *Why Johnny still can't Read.* New York: Harper and Row.

FRIES, C. (1962). *Linguistics and Reading.* New York: Holt, Rinehart and Winston.

FRITH, U. (1986). *Cognitive Processes in Spelling.* New York: Academic Press.

FUDGE, E.C. (1969). Syllables. *Journal of Linguistics,* **5**: 523.

GARDNER, M. (1970). *The Ambidextrous Universe: Left, Right and the Fall of Parity.* Pelican.

GELB, I.J. (1963). *A Study of Writing* (revised edition). Chicago, IL: University of Chicago Press.

GIBSON, E.J. (1971). Perceptual learning and the theory of word perception. *Cognitive Psychology,* **2**: 351–368.

GIBSON, E.J. AND LEVIN, H. (1975). *The Psychology of Reading.* Cambridge, MA: MIT Press.

GIBSON, E., ET AL. (1962) 'The role of Grapheme-Phoneme Correspondence in the Perception of Words' *American Journal of Psychology,* **75**: 554.

GIMSON, A.C. (1962). *An Introduction to the Pronunciation of English.* London: Arnold.

GOLDBERG, ET AL. (1983). *Dyslexia: interdisciplinary approaches to reading disability.* New York: Grune and Stratton.

GOODMAN, K.S. (1982). Reading: a psycholinguistic guessing game. In Gallasch, F.V. (Ed.), *Language and Literacy: the selected writings of Kenneth S. Goodman,* Vol.1. London: Routledge and Kegan Paul.

GOUGH, P.B. (1972). One second of reading. In Kavanagh, J.F. and Mattingley, I.G. (Eds) *Language by Ear and Eye.* Cambridge, MA: MIT Press.

HALL, R.A. (1960). A theory of graphemics. *Acta Linguistica,* **8**.

HAMPSHIRE, S. (1981). *Susan's Story.* London: Sidgwick and Jackson.

HEATON, P. (1996) *Parents in Need.* London: Whurr Publishers.

HENDERSON, L. (1982). *Orthography and Word Recognition in Reading.* London: Academic Press.

HORNSBY, B. and SHEAR, F. (1974). *Alpha to Omega: the A-Z of teaching reading, writing and spelling.* London: Heinemann Educational Books.

HUEY, E.B. (1908). *The Psychology and Pedagogy of Reading.* Cambridge, MA: MIT Press Edition, 1968.

JAMES, W. (1892). *Psychology (Advanced Course,* Vols. 1 and 2). Cambridge, MA: Henry Holt and Co.

KAVANAGH, J.F. and MATTINGLEY, I.G. (1972). *Language by Ear and Eye.* Cambridge, MA.: MIT Press.

KAVANAGH, J.F. and VENEZKY, R.L. (Eds), (1980). *Orthography, Reading and Dyslexia.* Baltimore: New York: University Park Press.

KOHLERS, P.A. (1973). Three stages of reading. In Smith, F. (Ed.) *Psycholinguistics and Reading.* New York: Holt Rinehart and Winston.

LABOV, W. (1965). Stages in the acquisition of standard English. In Shuy, R.W. (Ed.) *Social Dialects and Language Learning.* National Council of Teachers of English (USA).

LIBERMAN, A.M., COOPER, F.S., SHANKWEILER, D. and STUDDERT-KENNEDY, M. (1967). Perception of the speech code. *Psychological Review,* **74**. 431–461.

LINDSAY, P.H. and NORMAN, D.A. (1977). *Human Information Processing.* New York: Academic Press.

LOVELL, K., GRAY, E. and OLIVER, D. (1964). A further study of some cognitive and other disabilities in backward readers of average non-verbal reasoning scores. *British Journal of Educational Psychology,* **34**: 58–64.

MACKAY, D. and THOMPSON, B. (1968). The initial teaching of reading and writing. Paper 3 in *Programme in Linguistics and English Teaching,* London: Longman.

MEEK, M., ET AL. (1983). *Achieving Literacy: longitudinal studies of adolescents learning to read.* London: Routledge and Kegan Paul.

MICHAEL, I. (1970). *English Grammatical Categories ... to 1800.* Cambridge: Cambridge University Press.

MILES, T.R. (1975). *The Dyslexic Child*. Hove: Priory Press.

MILES, T.R. (1983a). *Dyslexia, the Pattern of Difficulties*. Charles C. Thomas.

MILES, T.R. (1983b). *The Bangor Dyslexia Test*. Wisbech, Cambs: Learning Development Aids.

MONEY, J. (Ed.) (1962). *Reading Disability: progress and research needs in dyslexia*. Baltimore, MD: The John Hopkins Press.

MORGAN, W. PRINGLE (1896). A case of congenital word blindness. *British Medical Journal*, **2**: 1378.

MORRIS, J.M. (Ed.) (1972). *The First R: yesterday, today and tomorrow*. London: Ward Lock Educational.

MUTER, V. (1982). The relationship between definitions and assessment in dyslexia. *Dyslexia Review*, **5**(1): 13–15.

NEWTON, M., THOMPSON, M.E., RICHARDS, I.L. (1979). *Readings in Dyslexia*. Wisbech: LDA.

NORRIS, E. *The Edith Norrie Letter Case*. Obtainable from the Helen Arkell Dyslexia Centre.

OGDEN, C.K. and RICHARDS, I.A. (1923). *The Meaning of Meaning*. London: Kegan Paul, Trench, Trubner and Co.

ORTON, S. (1937). *Reading, Writing and Speech Problems in Children*. London: Chapman and Hall.

PAVLIDIS, G.TH. and MILES, T.R. (Eds) (1981). *Dyslexia Research and its Applications to Education*. Chichester: John Wiley and Sons.

QUIRK, R., GREENBAUM, S., LEECH, G.N. and SVARTVIK, J. (1972). *A Grammar of Contemporary English*. London: Longman.

RUTTER, M., TIZZARD, J. and WHITMORE, K. (1970). *Education, Health and Behaviour*. London: Longman.

RUTTER, M. and SCHOPLER, E. (1978). *Autism, a Reappraisal of Concepts and Treatment*. New York: Plenum Press.

DE SAUSSURE, F. (1916). *Course in General Linguistics*. London: Collins, revised English Edition.

SHUY, R.W. (Ed.) (1965). *Social Dialects and Language. Learning*, National Council of Teachers of English, Bloomington, IN: Proceedings of Bloomington Conference.

SIMPSON, E. (1980). *Reversals: a personal account of victory over Dyslexia*. London: Gollancz.

SKEAT, W.W. (1882). *A Concise Etymological Dictionary of the English Language*. Oxford: Oxford University Press.

SMITH, F. (1980.) *Understanding Reading: a psycholinguistic account of reading and learning to read*. New York: Holt, Rinehart and Winston.

STEINHEISER, R. and GUTHRIE, J. (1974). Scanning times through prose and word strings for various targets by normal and disabled readers. *Perceptual and Motor Skills*, **39**: 931–938.

STRANG, B. (1962). *Modern English Structure*. London: Arnold.

STUBBS, M. (1980). *Language and Literacy: the socio-linguistics of reading and writing*. London: Routledge and Kegan Paul.

TAYLOR, I. (1883). *The Alphabet. An account of the origin and development of letters* (2 vols). London: Kegan Paul, Trench and Co.

THOMSON, M. (1984). *Developmental Dyslexia: its nature, assessment and remediation*. London: Edward Arnold.

THORNDIKE, E.L. AND LORGE, I. (1963). *The Teacher's Wordbook of 30,000 Words*. New York: Columbia University, Teachers' College.

TRUDGILL, P. (1974). *Sociolinguistics, an Introduction*. Pelican.

VELLUTINO, F.R. (1979). *Dyslexia Theory and Research*. Cambridge, MA: MIT Press.

VENEZKY, R.L. (1970). *The Structure of English Orthography*. The Hague: Mouton.

VENEZKY, R.L. (1976). *Theoretical and Experimental Base for Teaching Reading*. The Hague: Mouton.

WARNOCK, H.M. (1978.) *Special Educational Needs: report of the Ccommittee of Inquiry into the Education of Handicapped Children and Young People*. DES Comd. 7212.

WECHSLER, D. (1949) Wechsler Intelligence Scale for Children, New York: Psychological Corporation.

WELLS, J.C. AND COLSON, G. (1974). *Practical Phonetics*. London: Pitman.

WENDON, L. (1984). *Pictogram Supplies*. Cambridge: Barton.

WIJK, A. (1966). *Rules of Pronunciation for the English Language*. Oxford: Oxford University Press.

WINTERSON, P.S. (1981). *Rhythms and Tunes of English*. Exeter: University of Exeter (Exeter Tapes series).

WINTERSON, P.S. (1983). *Phonemic Transcription of English*. Exeter: University of Exeter (Exeter Tapes series).

WOLFF, A. (1973). *The Assessment and Teaching of Dyslexic Children*. London: The Invalid Children's Aid Association.

Select list of works consulted for the second edition

ADAMS, M.J. (1990). *Beginning to Read: the new phonics in context* (précis of fuller treatment published 1990 by MIT. Press).

AUGUR, J. *Children's Written Language Difficulties*. London: NFER/Nelson. (Edit) Snowling.

BARRON, R. and BARON, J. (1977). *How children get meaning from printed words*. Child Development, **48**: 587–594.

BERTELSON, P. (1986). The onset of literacy: liminal remarks. *Cognition* , **24**: 1–30.

BRADLEY, L. and BRYANT, P.E. (1983). Categorising sounds and learning to read: a causal connection. *Nature*, **301**: 419–421.

BRYANT, P. (1990). *Children's Written Language Difficulties*. London: NFER/Nelson. (Edit) Snowling.

FRITH, U. and SNOWLING, M. (1983). Reading for meaning and reading for sound in autistic and dyslexic children. *British Journal of Developmental Psychology*, **1**: 329–342.

GATES, A.I. and CHASE, E.H. (1926). Methods and theories of learning to spell tested by studies of deaf children. *Journal of Educational Psychology*, **17**: 289–300.

GLEITMAN, L.R. and ROZIN, P. (1977). The structure and acquisition of reading I: Relations between orthographies and the structure of language. In Reber, A.S. and Scarborough, D.L. (Eds) *Toward a Psychology of Reading* (pp. 1– 53). Hillsdale, NJ: Lawrence Erlbaum.

GOSWAMI, U. and BRYANT, P. (1990). *Phonological Skills and Learning to Read*. Hillsdale, NJ: Lawrence Erlbaum.

GOSWAMI, U. (1988). Orthographic analogies and reading development. *Quarterly Journal of Experimental Child Psychology*, **40A**: 239–268.

GOSWAMI, U. (1990). Phonological priming and orthographic analogies in reading. *Journal of Experimental Child Psychology*, **49**: 323–340.

HERDER, J.G. (1772). *Essay on the Origin of Language* (Translated by J.M. Moran and A. Gode). Frederick Ungar Publishing Co.

LEFOY, R. *Improving literacy through motor development*. Watford Dyslexia Unit, South Oxhey WD1 5HN

LIBERMAN, I.Y. (1982). *A language-oriented view of reading and its disabilities*. In Myklebust, H. (Ed.) *Progress in Learning Disabilities* (Vol. 5, pp. 81–101). New York: Grune and Stratton.

LIBERMAN, I.Y., SHANKWEILER, D., LIBERMAN, A.M., FOWLER, C and FISHER, F.W. (1977). Phonetic segmentation and recoding in the beginning reader. In Reber, A.S. and Scarborough, D.L. (Eds) *Toward a Psychology of Reading*. Hillsdale, NJ: Lawrence Erlbaum Associates.

LUNDBERG. I., FROST, J. and PETERSEN, O. (1988). Effects of an extensive program for stimulating phonological awareness in preschool children. *Reading Research Quarterly* , **23**: 263–284.

232

MORAIS, J., (1991). Metaphonological abilities and literacy. In Snowling, M. and
    Thomson, M. (Eds) *Dyslexia, Integrating Theory and Practice.* London: Whurr.

MORAIS, J., CARY, L., ALEGRIA, J. and BERTELSON, P. (1979). Does awareness of speech as
    a sequence of phones arise spontaneously? *Cognition,* **7**: 323–331.

Older and Younger, The Basic Skills of Different Age Groups. London: ALBSU (1995).

PERFETTI, C.A., BECK, I., BELL, L.C. and HUGHES, C. (1987). Phonemic knowledge and
    learning to read are reciprocal: a longitudinal study of first grade children. *Merrill-
    Palmer Quarterly,* **33**: 283–219.

ROZIN, P. and GLEITMAN, L.R. (1977). The structure and acquisition of reading II: The
    reading process and the acquisition of the alphabetic principle. In Reber, A.S. and
    Scarborough, D.L. (Eds) *Toward a Psychology of Reading* (pp. 55–141). Hillsdale, NJ:
    Lawrence Erlbaum.

SHANKWEILER, D. and CRAIN, S. (1986). Language mechanisms and reading disorder: a
    modular approach. *Cognition,* **24**: 139–168.

SNOWLING, M.J. (1980). The development of grapheme–phoneme correspondence in
    normal and dyslexic readers. *Journal of Experimental Child Psychology,* **29**.

SNOWLING, M. (1987). *Dyslexia: a cognitive developmental perspective.* Oxford: Basil Blackwell.

SNOWLING, M. and HULME, C. (1983). Developmental dyslexia and language disorders. In
    Blanken, G. et al. (Eds) *Linguistic Disorders and Pathologies* .Walter de Gruyter.

SNOWLING, M. and THOMSON, M. (Eds) (1991). *Dyslexia: integrating theory and practice.*
    London: Whurr.

STANOVICH, K.E. (1994). Does dyslexia exist? *Journal of Child Psychology and Psychiatry and
    Allied Disciplines,* **35** (4).

STUART, M. and COLTHEART M. (1988). Does reading develop in a succession of stages?
    Cognition, **30**: 139–181

TREIMAN, R. (1985). Onsets and rimes as units of spoken syllables: evidence from chil-
    dren. *Journal of Experimental Child Psychology,* **39**: 161–81.

TUNMER, W.E., HERRIMAN, M.L. and NESDALE, A.R. (1988). Metalinguistic abilities and
    beginning reading. *Reading Research Quarterly,* **23**: 134–58.

VAN DER WISSEL, A. and ZEGERS, F.E. (1985).Reading retardation revisited. *British Journal
    of Developmental Psychology,* **3**: 3–9.

Appendix A
The BDA Diploma
Reading List

ADAMS, M.J. (1990). *Beginning to Read*. Cambridge, MA: MIT Press.

BADDELEY, A. *Your Memory – A User's Guide*. Harmondsworth: Penguin Books.

BRADLEY, L. (1980). *Assessing Reading Difficulties*. Windsor: NFER/Nelson.

BRITISH PSYCHOLOGICAL SOCIETY. *Phonological Assessment of Specific Learning Difficulties*. Edited by Norah Fredrickson, Rea Reason (Educational and Child Psychology). BPS Books, 48 Princes Road East, Leicester LE1 7DR.

BRITISH PSYCHOLOGICAL SOCIETY. *Open Learning Units*. BPS Books, 48 Princes Road East, Leicester LE1 7DR.

BRITISH PSYCHOLOGICAL SOCIETY. *Introduction to Cognitive Processes*. Nicky Hayes. BPS Books, 48 Princes Road East, Leicester LE1 7DR.

BRITISH PSYCHOLOGICAL SOCIETY. *Remembering and Forgetting*. Annette Cassells. BPS Books, 48 Princes Road East, Leicester LE1 7DR.

BRITISH PSYCHOLOGICAL SOCIETY. *Thinking and Problem Solving*. Philip Banyard and Nicky Hayes. BPS Books, 48 Princes Road East, Leicester LE1 7DR.

BRITISH PSYCHOLOGICAL SOCIETY. *Attention and Skills Learning*. Peter Reddy. BPS Books, 48 Princes Road East, Leicester LE1 7DR.

BRITISH PSYCHOLOGICAL SOCIETY. *Language and Thought*. Judith Hartland. BPS Books, 48 Princes Road East, Leicester LE1 7DR.

BRYANT, P. and Bradley, L. (1985). *Children's Reading Problems*. Oxford: Blackwell.

CHALL, J. (1983). *Stages of Reading Development*. Maidenhead: McGraw/Hill.

CHASTY, H. and FRIEL, J. (1981). *Children with Special Needs, Assessment, Law and Practice – Caught in the Act*. London: Jessica Kingsley.

CHINN, S.J. and ASHCROFT, J.R. *Mathematics for Dyslexics: A Teaching Handbook*. London: Whurr Publishers.

CLAY, M. (1979). *The Early Detection of Reading Difficulties*. Oxford: Heinemann.

CLAY, M. (1991). *Becoming Literate*. Oxford: Heinemann.

CRYSTAL, D. *Children's Language*. Harlow: Longman.

CRYSTAL, D. *Introduction to Language Pathology*. Hodder.

DAY, J. *A Software Guide for Specific Learning Difficulties*. National Council for Educational Technology.

DOCKRELL and McSHANE (1993). *Children's Learning Difficulties – A Cognitive Approach*. Oxford: Blackwell.

DAYAN, G. (1992). *Clearing the Way – The Dyslexia and Technology Pocket Book*. Day Video, South Shields.

EDWARDS, J. (1994). *The Scars of Dyslexia*. London: Cassell.

EKINSMYTH and BYNNER (1994). *The Basic Skills of Young Adults*. London: ALBSU.

ELLIS, A. (1984). *Reading, Writing and Dyslexia*. Hove: Lawrence Erlbaum.

FARNHAM-DIGGORY, S. *Learning Difficulties*. Fontana/Open Books.

FONTANA, D. (1988). *Psychology for Teachers*. BPS in association with MacMillan.

FRITH, U. (1990). *Cognitive Processes in Spelling*. London: Academic Press.

GALABURDA, A. (1993). *Dyslexia and Development: Neurobiological Aspects of Extraordinary Brains*. Harvard University Press.

GARDNER, H. (1993). *Frames of Mind – The Theory of Intelligence*. Fontana.

GOSWAMI and BRYANT, P. (1990). *Phonological Skills and Learning to Read*. Hove: Lawrence Erlbaum.

HALES, G. *Dyslexia Matters*. London: Whurr Publishers.

HENDERSON, A. *Maths and Dyslexics*. St Davids College, Llandudno.

HULME, C. and SNOWLING, M.J. (1994). *Reading Development and Dyslexia*. London: Whurr Publishers.

HYND, G. and COHEN, M. (1993). *Dyslexia: Neurological Theory, Research and Clinical Differentiation*. Gruner Stratton.

LUNZER, E. and GARDNER, K. (1979). *The Effective Use of Reading*. Harlow: Oliver and Boyd.

LUNZER, E. and GARDNER, K. (1984). *Learning from the Written Word*. Harlow: Oliver and Boyd.

McKEOWN (1992). *IT Support for Specific Learning Difficulties*. National Council for Educational Technology.

McLOUGHLIN, D., FITZGIBBON, G. and YOUNG, V. (1993). *Adult Dyslexia: Assessment, Counselling and Training*. London: Whurr Publishers.

MILES and GILROY. *Dyslexia at College*. London: Routledge.

MILES and MILES (1990). *Dyslexia A 100 Years On*. Buckingham: Open University Press.

MILLAR, R. and KLEIN, C. *Making Sense of Spelling*. Language and Literacy Unit, Southwark College, Asylum Road, London SE15 2RJ.

MOGFORD and SADLER. *Child Language Disability*. Vol 1 Implications in an Educational Setting (1989). Vol 2 Semantic and Pragmatic Difficulties. Vol 3 Hearing Impairment (1993). Clevedon, Avon: Multilingual Matters Ltd.

PAVLIDIS, G. and MILES, T. (1981). *Dyslexia Research and its Application to Education*. Chichester: Wiley.

PAVLIDIS, G. and FISHER (1986). *Dyslexia: Neuropsychology and Treatment*. Chichester: Wiley.

PUMPHREY, P. and ELLIOT, C. (1990). *Children's Difficulties in Reading, Writing and Spelling*. Basingstoke: Falmer Press.

PUMPHREY, P. and REASON (1991). *Specific Learning Difficulties (Dyslexia)*. London: Routledge.

REID, G. (1994). *Specific Learning Difficulties (Dyslexia) – A Handbook for Study and Practice*. Edinburgh: Moray House.

SASSOON, R. (1988). *The Practical Guide to Children's Handwriting*. London: Thames and Hudson.

SHARRON, H. (1987). *Changing Children's Minds*. London: Souvenir Press.

SLOBADA, J. (1985). *The Musical Mind – The Cognitive Psychology of Music*. Oxford: OUP.

SMITH and BLOOR (1985). *Simple Phonetics for Teachers*. London: Routledge.

SNOWLING, M. (1985). *Children's Written Language Difficulties*. London: Routledge.

SNOWLING, M. *Dyslexia: A Cognitive Developmental Perspective*. Oxford: Blackwell.

SNOWLING, M. and THOMSON, M. (1991). *Dyslexia: Integrating Theory and Practice*. London: Whurr Publishers.

STIRLING, E. (1985). *Help for the Dyslexic Adolescent*. Stirling.

TEMPLE, C. (1993). *The Brain – An Introduction to the Psychology of the Human Brain and Behaviour*. Harmondsworth: Penguin.

THOMPSON, TUNMER and NICHOLSON (1993). *Reading Acquisition Processes*. Clevedon, Avon: Multilingual Matters Ltd.

THOMSON, M. (1989). *Developmental Dyslexia, 3rd Edition*. London: Whurr Publishers.

THOMSON, M. and WATKINS, W. (1990). *Dyslexia: A Teaching Handbook*. London: Whurr Publishers.

VELLUTINO, F. *Dyslexia: Theory and Research*. Cambridge, MA: MIT Press.

WELLS, J.C. and COLSON, G. *Practical Phonetics*. London: Pitman.

WEST, T. (1991). *In the Mind's Eye*. Prometheus Books.

ADDRESSES

Adult Dyslexia Organisation
336 Brixton Road
London
SW9 7AA

British Dyslexia Association
98 London Road
Reading
RG1 5AU

British Psychological Association
St Andrews House
48 Princes Road East
Leicester
LE1 7DR

Dyslexia Computer Resource Centre
Department of Psychology
University of Hull
Hull
HU6 7RX

Helen Arkell Dyslexia Centre
14 Crondace Road
London
SW6 4BB

Invalid Children's Aid Association
126 Buckingham Palace Road
London
SW1 9SB

LDA Living and Learning
Duke Street
Wisbech
Cambridgeshire
PE13 2AE

Special Education Needs Marketing
9 The Close
Church Ashton
Newport
TF10 9JL

Appendix B
44 Significant Sound Units of English

Vowels

A sound unit rendered by its phonemic symbol	A word containing the same sound unit	The same word in phonemic symbols
1 æ	bag	bæg
2 ɛ	beg	bɛg
3 ɪ	list	lɪst
4 ɒ	pond	pɒnd
5 ʌ	bung	bʌŋ
6 ʊ	push	pʊʃ
7 eɪ	pay	peɪ
8 i	mean	min
9 aɪ	guy	gaɪ
10 əʊ	own	əʊn
11 u	do	du
12 ɑ	half	hɑf
13 ɔ	gnaw	nɔ
14 ɜ	purr	pɜ
15 ɔɪ	join	dʒɔɪn
16 ɪə	sneer	snɪə
17 ɛə	chair	tʃɛə
18 ɑʊ	now	nɑʊ
19 ə	about	əbaʊt

Consonants

A sound…	A word…	The same word…
20 b	bite	baɪt
21 p	put	pʊt
22 t	test	tɛst
23 d	dream	drim
24 k	keen	kin
25 ʷk	queen	ʷkin
26 g	good	gʊd
27 ʃ	sugar	ʃʊgə
28 ʒ	pleasure	plɛʒə
29 tʃ	chalk	tʃɔk
30 dʒ	jet	dʒɛt
31 h	hit	hɪt
32 f	fight	faɪt
33 v	vast	vɑst
34 θ	thing	θɪŋ
35 ð	though	ðəʊ
36 s	swim	swɪm
37 z	zest	zɛst
38 m	meat	mit
39 n	gnat	næt
40 ŋ	sing	sɪŋ
41 l	leap	lip
42 r	red	rɛd
43 j	yacht	jɒt
44 w	watch	wɒtʃ

vocalic l and n occur as in
bɒtḷ (bottle) and bʌtṇ (button)

Throughout this book <word> means 'written word', /word/ means 'spoken word'. For full discussion of phonemic symbols etc. see Book 3

Appendix C
Game IX (Revision)

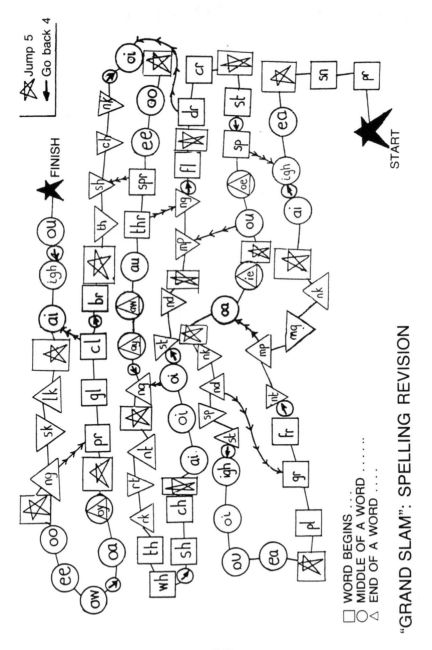

Jump 5
Go back 4

FINISH

START

☐ WORD BEGINS .....
☐◯ MIDDLE OF A WORD ....
◁ END OF A WORD .....

"GRAND SLAM": SPELLING REVISION

240

Index